TRUTH *and* DARE

DARING TO LIVE YOUR TRUTH IN A FAKE WORLD

BY

WENDY BUNNELL

TRUTH and DARE
DARING TO LIVE YOUR TRUTH IN A FAKE WORLD

Copyright © 2022 by Wendy Bunnell

All rights reserved. No part of this publication may be reproduced, stored in a retrieval system, or transmitted in any form or by any means, electronic, mechanical, photocopying, recording, or otherwise, without written permission of the publisher or author, except for the use of brief quotations in a book review.

Although the author and publisher have made every effort to ensure that the information in this book was correct at press time, the author and publisher do not assume and hereby disclaim any liability to any party for any loss, damage, or disruption caused by errors or omissions, whether such errors or omissions result from negligence, accident, or any other cause.

Adherence to all applicable laws and regulations, including international, federal, state and local governing professional licensing, business practices, advertising, and all other aspects of doing business in the US, Canada or any other jurisdiction is the sole responsibility of the reader and consumer.

Neither the author nor the publisher assumes any responsibility or liability whatsoever on behalf of the consumer or reader of this material. Any perceived slight of any individual or organization is purely unintentional.

The resources in this book are provided for informational purposes only and should not be used to replace the specialized training and professional judgment of a health care or mental health care professional.

Neither the author nor the publisher can be held responsible for the use of the information provided within this book. Please always consult a trained professional before making any decision regarding treatment of yourself or others.

To request permissions, contact the publisher at
contact@freedomhousepublishingco.com or wendy@wendybunnell.com

Paperback ISBN: 978-1-952566-90-5
Ebook ISBN: 978-1-952566-89-9
Printed in the USA.

Freedom House Publishing Co
Meridian, ID 83646
www.freedomhousepublishingco.com

DEDICATION

This book is dedicated to those that feel their heart strings pulling them toward a more expansive way of living and loving. To those that hear the war cry of the heart.

This is for you . . .

TABLE OF CONTENTS

Dedication iii
Preface: Before the truth was found… vii
Chapter 1: The Journey to Truth 1
Chapter 2: Truth about Fear and Love 13
Chapter 3: Truth about the Body 23
Chapter 4: Truth about Intuition 37
Chapter 5: Truth about Emotion 53
Chapter 6: Truth about Feminine and Masculine Energy 65
Chapter 7: Truth about Breath 77
Chapter 8: Truth about Meditation 89
Chapter 9: Truth about Prayer 99
Chapter 10: Truth about Relationships 109
Chapter 11: Truth about Religion 119
Chapter 12: Truth about Money 133
Chapter 13: Truth about Sex 149
Chapter 14: Truth about Trauma 159
Chapter 15: Truth about Plant Medicine 169
Chapter 16: Truth about the Present 179
Chapter 17: Truth about Surrender 189
Chapter 18: Truth about Forgiveness 199

Chapter 19: Truth about Judgment 209
Chapter 20: Truth Found 217
Poem: The Warrior Cry of the Heart 225
Prologue 227
Truth & Dare Resources 231
Acknowledgements 233
About the Author 235

Preface
BEFORE THE TRUTH WAS FOUND...

A letter to my wounded heart...a letter to all of the wounded hearts in the world . . .

I see you. I see beyond the exterior smile. Behind the façade of happiness lies the weary. Behind the excited lies the tired. Behind the smile lies the pain.

I am here with you, wrapping you up in a warm blanket of support, love, and understanding.

You have been on a long journey of pain and the inner chaos is stifling.

You are tired. You are weary. You are done.

Some days, you may not even feel like you can breathe. The suffocation that you are feeling disconnects you from everything. Even when you are with the ones you love, you don't feel like you can find it anymore.

Where did it go?

Even though there are momentary glimpses of happiness, it seems like you start to find it and then it slips through your fingers once again.

And you wonder why. Why does it seem to go so fast and the darkness sets in right behind it so very quickly. Why doesn't this happiness stay? Why does it run away from you?

You have tried everything imaginable. You have read positive books, listened to podcasts on how to improve your life to become a better parent, spouse, lover, business person, friend, and tried out this connection-with-self thing that the gurus are telling you will make it all better.

So far, nothing has worked well. They may have improved something slightly. But nothing sticks.

And you wonder what is wrong with you. Why can everyone else figure this out and you are left hanging and trying to discover the missing link that may set you free?

There has to be freedom somewhere, otherwise this life is simply to be endured instead of enjoyed. And someone said that it can be enjoyed?

But you don't know where that exists.

You know the pain. You know the darkness.

Pain is what you know really well, and it seems like the only thing that stays.

You still worry about everything: money, relationships, children, the endless to-do list.

Darkness and depression seem to be the friends that hang out the most and linger in your heart for hours. They keep you up at night as you ruminate over the stress and worry and strife that exists in your life.

You may even have one part of your life figured out. Maybe you're a great business person and the money is flowing to you. Or perhaps you have hobbies that bring you joy and something to look forward to. Maybe you work out every day and take pride in the incredible physique you have created.

But yet there is still something missing. Those things bring temporary joy and then leave as fast as they came. And somewhere in your existence you feel this pull toward the truth. It's out there somewhere.

I get you.

I see you.

I relate.

I may even understand parts of your life.

And I want to embrace you in this tender circle of love that assures you that maybe that yearning to search for more can actually be satisfied.

I recall a few years ago sitting on the floor of my son's home and wrestling with my grandchildren on the floor. I felt like I was observing from afar. I saw this woman in my vision that appeared to be having such a great time, laughing and loving and experiencing connection with her grandkids. From the outside it appeared that I had a beautiful existence and was enjoying the amazing moments we are given in our lives.

And yet all I felt was numb. I was numb to love, numb to joy, numb to this existence that kept getting more challenging every day.

I put on a happy face and dove into doing more. Because if I do more, maybe I will feel more.

Maybe I will feel something, anything. Anything but this dark cloud of fear that has wedged itself into every molecule in my being.

Please God, please let me feel something besides pain and stress. Help me have joy and happiness for more than an hour here and there or a day at a time.

It has to be out there.

It must be out there.

It has to be found or I don't want this life. I don't care about the lessons and the reason I was sent here to begin with, whatever that may be. I simply want to feel love and safety once again, because I don't feel safe.

I feel anything but safe.

Do you feel anything but safe too?

My dear brother and sister, I lovingly see you with a heart that understands. I desire to help you see the truth once more, because once you experience it again, you will know where to find it. It becomes easier and easier to access until it becomes the new version of you—the only version of you that has ever existed since the beginning of time.

This darkness that has pervaded your soul isn't real. It isn't truth and it has marinated into every aspect of your life and taken over *you* until you can't see anything else but this feeling. It has infected relationships, abundance, experiences, and rest and relaxation. In fact, you may wonder what it means to relax, because even when you do sit down and try to "chill," you can't seem to get there anymore. There are too many thoughts and unsettling things that cover your spirit in a black sea of fear.

My only prayer is that you will accept this offer for a seed of hope.

Start with that.

Consider that there may be answers out there.

Yes, I know you have tried. I know you have read books, attended seminars, dived into your religious practices, asked people who have what you think may bring you peace, and you have found some healing, but it is always there underneath. The roots are planted firmly and you would pull them out, but you don't know where to start pulling.

Come with me for a few hours and I will walk you to the place that needs your first attention. We will pull out those weeds of fear and replace them with flowers of love, peace, and joy.

And you can have them for much more than a few hours or a few days at a time. In fact, you will remember and feel like you have awakened from a deep slumber, that the life you have created has been based on the programs, stories, and beliefs that weren't of your conscious making.

Once you know, you can consciously re-create. You can remember where to access answers and love and truth in every single moment of your life. And in that remembering, it will feel like miracles encircle you, astounding you with things that could never have been just "coincidence." And after a while, you will recognize that these aren't necessarily miracles, but just the new world that was there; you simply couldn't see it anymore.

The only way there is through. The only way to see is to unsee. The only way to feel positive is to make peace with the negative. And it isn't as hard as you might think it will be. In fact, it is the most natural thing in the world, once you remember and start to see things unfold in the truth of what they have always been.

I know the entire world is in chaos right now.

I am not living a Pollyanna existence.

I see what is happening. I celebrate what is happening.

We can relate to the state of affairs in the world, but we can unravel the fear and oppression that they are allowing to come into our awareness and making us so uncomfortable that we are willing to do anything to feel safe once again.

Thank them.

They are here to bring you back to the truth.

Because when no one else can provide the answers you are seeking, and you have tried everything else out there, you will get down on your knees to figure this life out. The recipe and protocols that you have tried haven't worked. In fact, they have convinced you that the answers to your issues will be found outside of you. And when you become teachable and humble and like a little child, you are in a place to discover and be gently awakened to that familiar knowing, to that familiar feeling of connection and love and joy.

Fear will be a teacher and love will be your new mantra.

Welcome home. Welcome home to you. Welcome to your truth.

Chapter 1
THE JOURNEY TO TRUTH

I walked up the stairs to the stargazing deck. It is just large enough to house two lounging chairs and a small patio set. Even though it was designed for a person to look at the stars, it was morning and I had climbed to the top to look over the entire valley.

It was absolutely breathtaking. I took in every shade of burnt orange, and the deep green cedar trees giving dimension to the sea of red over the valley, a sharp contrast to the endless blue skies. The ethereal clouds were moving ever so slowly, morphing in and out of shapes as they flowed past my vision. The sun was just peeking over the horizon and displaying its splendor of colors as it fulfilled its promise of a new day.

I rolled out my yoga mat and started moving with the music and my breath. I could feel the familiar feeling of my spirit, mind, and body forming a union as I flowed in and out of the sun salutations and postures that always take me out of hearing the never-ending dialogue in my head.

I finished my practice in Savasana and dipped down into that place of peace that I know so well now.

It's a familiarity that I have known this feeling my entire existence.

And a stream of memories passed by my consciousness.

Memories of me pleading for something different, crying for a way out of the misery that I felt in every area of my life.

I saw myself walking down the aisle at my wedding and feeling like I was attending my funeral instead of my wedding.

I saw myself frustrated and broken as I held my firstborn son and didn't know how I was ever going to manage being a mother at the age of nineteen.

Another memory filtered through, one of me lying in bed awake as I stressed and worried about how we were going to pay bills and afford food.

Yet another of me begging God to help me find a way out of my marriage.

My body was riddled with chronic pain that no doctor, no drug, no supplement, no modality could take away.

Now the memories started rushing by at a faster pace: my father dying of a drug overdose, losing a baby to miscarriage, my sister losing her twin babies, my son trying to commit suicide, my children struggling with life, my husband losing his job, deep depression and anxiety crippling my world, my body slowly dying, my leaving my faith of origin, my endless crying and hurting.

As I came back to reality, it dawned on me that everything I had agonized and begged to be released from had become my current reality and had manifested in real time . . .

My body is healthy once again.

My dream relationship, the same one I had begged to be free of, now brings me more joy than I can verbally express.

My crippling anxiety and depression are no longer my story.

I have learned that financial abundance is my birthright.

My children are living their own journey and I cheer from the sidelines instead of rescuing.

Joy and happiness take the place of the grief and sorrow that used to be my existence.

I realize that the chapters of this book have healed the last shards of pain in my life.

I am free.

I am joyful.

I am my truth.

The book you hold in your hands shows the way through the pain I experienced most of my life and how I came out the other side. Some of the principles and healing came through writing the information channeled to me from a source much greater than myself. I didn't even know the principles prior to embarking on the journey of writing this book.

I know these principles work, because I am living proof that they do.

While my life hasn't always been completely bleak and miserable, I lived some of my life in a sea of despair. It was hard to feel love because there was too much pain blocking it from being received.

Until now.

You will discover that I teach through my stories.

They are what I know best.

They are the only stories in which I can remember with all of my five senses and share how I learned spiritual truths that apply to all of humanity. And so that is where I will come from.

And even though they won't be your stories, we can relate through the same emotions that we both understand, the same insecurities, and much of the same beliefs that we formed at a young age.

You will understand them because we have a universal language of love that doesn't change. We understand what love is because it is the most natural thing in the world to feel it.

This book is all about opening your heart and allowing it to receive and give love. Opening our hearts is the most important thing we do in this lifetime. When we can learn to live our lives with an open heart, we will experience the full power and potential of this lifetime. We will have energy, vitality, joy, bliss, and experiences that will remind us of our true nature. It is only when we close our hearts that we continually feel pain and suffering.

That is basically what happened in my transformation.

I closed my heart in the trauma, and didn't open it back up until I got to a point where I couldn't do this life anymore.

In fact, I recall telling my very first story (not that many years ago), which was the beginning of my healing.

I had just attended a few conferences that helped plant the seed of hope that I could create my own life, and that it wasn't left simply to fate. I remember how powerful that made me feel and how that buzzed with truth throughout my whole being.

I felt this gentle nudge that I had something uniquely mine that I could offer to help others while helping myself at the same time—that this special spiritual gift would bring more purpose and satisfaction than anything else. And I understand that when our will aligns with Source Energy, we begin to feel that peace and clarity we have been searching for.

So I started asking around. I wanted to know how I could serve and what unique role I could play in this lifetime.

I started to ask folks, what am I good at? What is something that comes effortlessly to me?

The answer?

"You talk a lot."

Wow! Thank you folks. I sure appreciate that.

Talking has brought me a lot of grief in my life. I remember my father saying that he took me on a business trip that was six hours away and that I talked the WHOLE TIME both there and back. My talking was the innocent butt of jokes for a very long time, but I always wondered if there was something wrong with me. This was the beginning of a story that I would later form a belief around.

Yep—I have the gift of gab. And in junior high, I finally made the drill team and found my love for dance. We had requirements to dance in each performance and that was all tied to our report card. I remember holding my breath each time I received my report card. Not because of academic grades, but because of citizenship grades. I would scan over the card quickly, looking for the 1s, 2s and 3s. The 1s were what I was shooting for. They were what allowed me to dance and enjoy the fruits of my hard work. The 2s meant I needed to work on my behavior and would mean that I sat out one game. The 3s meant that I had serious behavior issues and I wouldn't be allowed to dance for two games.

I would scan over the report card and each time I would see . . . 1,1,2,2,1,3.

Dang!! I couldn't shut the yap trap! I would end up sitting on the stands more often than dancing on the field, all because of my mouth.

So I shut up.

In high school, I didn't talk much. I sat on the sidelines and behaved as I should. I didn't hang out with many high school kids and preferred to party with the college-aged kids.

I was too much, I was too loud, and I needed to blend in with the crowd to be accepted.

And now everyone was saying that my skill was speaking?

So I turned to another resource. I had received a special blessing when I was around twenty-four years old. That blessing identified things that would help me to live the best life I could while here on Earth.

I read over it once again to see what it might say. As I read the words, "You have the gift of communication. You have the ability to use words so that others can understand truth," I cried tears of joy and understanding. My gift of gab was not a curse, but a true blessing that, once harnessed, could help so many others.

The trick was getting out there and doing it—using my gift to help others

It was probably the first "God dare" that I actually took.

I knew that a friend was organizing a women's conference in our town and I offered to help in exchange for the opportunity to speak in a breakout session.

That would be my first speaking opportunity . . . ever.

As I walked into the room, I noticed that it was standing room only. The topic I had chosen seemed to resonate with others. The title of my address was "Critical to Confidence," turning that negative voice into a voice of love toward ourselves. Once again I would teach through stories, using my story as a vehicle for understanding.

I shared my first lesson of understanding my truth. This was the beginning. This is the way God teaches me: I have an experience, I learn a lesson, and then I solidify that lesson by teaching it to others. It's in this manner that what I learn becomes a part of me.

My first lesson included gratitude. At one point in my life, I perceived my world as crumbling around me. I had identified myself as being a mother first and foremost above all other titles. And because I was looking for external validation for my worth, how my family was doing determined my worth

I did pretty well while the kids were little and I was calling the shots. It was when they got older and started to make mistakes—as humans will do—that my philosophy of life got shaken to its core.

My oldest child was addicted to drugs and getting in trouble with the law, my daughter was pregnant with a special-needs child, and my third child was being threatened with being kicked out of school because of serious behavior problems. I looked lovingly down to my four-year-old and wondered how I would screw him up too, because the common denominator in all of their lives was that they had the same mother and the same father. Oh, no, Dad wasn't getting off the hook; he was part of the problem too and he was going down with me.

At one point, I truly convinced myself that my children would be better off being raised by another mother. The quote, "No success can compensate for failure in the home" recycled in my thoughts over and over, convincing me that I was beyond repair. In that moment, the only thing that proved to be a good thing was that I was compelled to kneel down and ask for help and guidance. I poured my heart and soul out to my creator, begging for solace and forgiveness. And as I quieted my mind, there was one word that came to me that would forever change my life.

The word was gratitude: love in action; perceiving what is instead of what isn't.

And honestly, I was ticked. I felt like I had been given a slap across the face. Why wasn't God comforting me and allowing me to feel immediate relief? Gratitude—didn't He hear everything I had just said?

I got nothing.

Nothing to be grateful for—my life is in the toilet and I messed it up beyond repair.

The only thing that I could hold onto is that I had heard that voice. I heard it and I couldn't deny that I was valuable enough for guidance to filter in.

Maybe it did matter. Maybe my existence was purposeful.

And things started to shift. I started to see things differently, and perceive the beauty instead of the darkness.

I noticed my little boy smiling at me and saying at least five times per day, "*Sigh . . .Mom, I wuv you."

I noticed the sunset and the mountains and the moments of bliss once again.

That is where it started.

It started with gratitude as my first lesson. Once I felt gratitude, I was open to all of the other truths as I was ready for them.

I end that story with the celebrations of discovering the real truth. When gratitude filled my heart, I learned how to perceive things differently and to understand that everything in my life was there for my highest and best good. There wasn't a punishment or a consequence because I wasn't worthy to receive anything other than that.

And the crowd in my breakout group at that conference cheered because they also felt those same feelings and had those same thoughts. We were tied together in a story that all of us had experienced. It was a story where we weren't enough, or we were too much, or we were messing up this thing called "life" because somehow we didn't know how to do it right.

So here I am again, teaching from a place of inner experience: my stories, my life, my perception.

As I offer these ideas, I know that I am living them. I will not offer anything that I don't know, that I don't feel, that I don't believe in my whole heart.

One of my other gifts is the gift of vulnerability. I am willing to get real so that you can too. In fact, there is one story in particular that I wrestled with and wasn't sure I wanted to share. But I choose to share it (in another chapter) in an effort to help—even if I help only one person with their own journey.

In this book, I am sharing my most private moments, thoughts, and tragedies so that I can set us all free.

I know this is possible because I have set myself free—free from the bondage that the external world set on me.

And now it is your turn.

You are on a discovery of truth.

You are about to embark on a journey back to yourself.

And the world isn't happy about this.

Because it has programmed you and me and everyone else to believe that we have to listen to them, to the voices around us, to the "experts," to the people who know more than we do.

But most likely, there has been something nagging at you for some time now. You may have caught glimpses of this inner voice from time to time, and in your soul you know that there is something more, something different. It is yearning to be heard, and so you feel this inner shift and a sense of urgency to go find out what that something is all about.

You just don't know where to stay in its presence. It seems to flit and flee every time you get close to it, and the barrage of chaos and clutter flitters back into your mind once again.

It is so noisy, so busy, and so distracting. All.the.time.

But here you are, reading this book, because that place inside of you led you here. At this time, and in this place, and in this realm, you are ready to peel back the layers that have been preventing you from knowing the truth.

"They" don't want you to know, because if you find yourself back in that truth, they will no longer have any control over you. The fear will dissipate and you will discover that all of the truth is inside, waiting for you to discover it.

The world has become increasingly noisy. If we rely on safety from the outside world, we will feel incredibly insecure during this time in the history of the world.

It doesn't take much to see that this world appears to be falling apart. Simply turn on the TV and watch the madness unfold right before your eyes.

The conflicting viewpoints leave us wondering who is telling the truth, what we should believe, and what is a lie. We worry about our economy, our families, our livelihood, and our very existence.

How can we get through life during this time?

What if I were to tell you that we live in the greatest time in all of human existence?

You would probably think that I am absolutely crazy and then tell me to pull my head out of the hippy sand I have it in.

I honestly believe with all my heart that we truly do—we live in the greatest time in all of human existence When we get to the point that we cannot and will not take advice from the outside world, we will dive into a place that has long been forgotten: that place that has always held the truth and the light that have been dimmed by the programs, beliefs, and stories that we made up about ourselves.

The breakdown always happens before the breakthrough.

The only way there is through—to plow through the bullshit we have built around our hearts and our spirits.

I am not going to promise a smooth road, but I will promise that traveling this road is worth it. I will promise that you will feel peace and joy and ecstasy that you never knew you could feel. I also promise that you will still get the opportunity to feel every emotion that this human body can feel.

And you might even celebrate it after you discover the tools to flow in and live life.

You may learn to accept sorrow, anxiety, anger, depression, and grief. You may allow them to *flow* through you instead of getting *stuck* in you.

So while life may not change externally, you will change internally, which changes everything.

You will never perceive anything the same ever again.

The truth will unfold.

The truth is inside of you.

It's time to step into the light. Are you ready?

Chapter 2

TRUTH ABOUT FEAR AND LOVE

The phone rang, I picked it up and heard my older sister crying. My sister never cries.

"Kellie, what is going on?"

"It's Dad. They found him in a hotel room. He died last night."

I heard my body start to make this noise that sounded like something between a laugh and a cry.

"Wendy, why are you laughing? Really?! This is real. Dad died last night!"

"I'm not laughing. I don't know what is going on, but I will call you later."

My body was responding but my mind hadn't caught up.

My Dad? My larger than life Dad? The one who would enter a room and command attention simply with his presence? That dad? The one who could take anything and turn it into gold? The one who helped start XM radio? The person who had the most infectious laugh, the most beautiful voice, and the most magnetic personality?

I couldn't and wouldn't accept it in that moment. He had been my hero in so many respects, and he had a heart of gold. I always knew he loved me and that he wished he could love everyone more.

But he had demons that followed him around, and they had pulled him down into the depths of hell one too many times in his lifetime. He had just been released from what may have been the twelfth rehab center and he went into a hotel room and overdosed.

The demons were his own thoughts, beliefs, and programs, but they had finally consumed his whole being.

And I grieved. I cried tears that I didn't think would ever stop. I felt this deep feeling of fear envelope me, threatening to overtake me.

In that grief I leaned into fear instead of love. I didn't even know it was something that I could consciously choose. I just knew that I would never be the same again.

This event led to me disconnecting from the last shards of my soul and heart. Each time I got a bit closer to connecting with my heart and soul, I would feel the pain of this event and other traumas in my life and I simply had to shut out the world.

The panic attacks started soon after my dad died.

The sleepless nights began. I would awaken from a dead sleep with my heart beating wildly, and then my mind would stop working. I felt like my body was overtaking me and I couldn't do anything about it. I didn't even know why it started most of the time because I usually wasn't stressed—or so I thought.

The first time it happened, I called my husband, who was on a shift with his job in law enforcement. He used his lights so he could race home and pick up his wife, who was surely having a heart attack and needing to go to the emergency room. In the ER, the nurse on duty seemed to be irritated that here was yet another person having a panic attack. She rolled her eyes and led me into a room and administered two Xanax to get my heart rate to calm down and get to a place of neutral.

But it was never neutral when I came back into my body. It was always dark. It was always depressing and black as tar.

And all I could do was go through the motions of taking care of my kids and working my job and doing the things that mothers do.

The joy had been taken and in its place were the pills that the doctor gave me to make it all go away.

And to me, that was better than feeling anything at all.

And so I took the pills for ten years and went through the motions of life, not really feeling pain, but certainly not feeling much joy, or any other emotion for that matter.

The fear had infected my soul. I allowed it to take over everything. And the story I created about walking a similar path to my father might have soon been realized if I didn't discover a way to lean back into love.

Thank goodness my soul kept nudging me to discover the truth.

The truth was inside: the truth that showed that I could return to love if I chose to do so. That I could experience a different way of being, but it was 100% my responsibility to get there. I had been searching for something different for so long. I knew that I wanted more than just a numb existence with an occasional moment of happiness, but I didn't know how to get it.

It would take me years to uncover one layer of lies after another. This doesn't mean it needs to take you years, but it took me decades. Regardless of how long it takes, it is worth every moment you can work toward the goal of rediscovering the love that will allow you to feel the joy and peace you have been searching for.

That is what we do in this lifetime. Every single thing we seek is in exchange for the "feeling" we think we will get when we achieve or receive it. We want a fancy car because we think it will make us feel accepted and loved. We want a high-paying job so we can purchase more of these items that will inevitably take the place of the gap in our souls.

We want a relationship that will fill us with love because we can't find it within ourselves. We want children that will fill us with purpose because we think that this role will seal up that hole in our hearts.

And while all of these things can give us some pleasure, each one has its pitfalls and can never be the constant source of happiness that we want so desperately.

And all of these unquenchable cravings for something outside of ourselves will prove to fall short in the end. They are designed to give us added value, but we must first feel whole before we experience the full joy and love that they can provide, because the never-ending source must be within instead of without.

And then there is love.

Fear and love. And all the emotions we experience can either be perceived in a loving manner or in a fearful manner. We can honor emotions such as anger if they help us get motivated to make some bold and courageous decisions, but those emotions can also move us into fear if we believe that they are bad and then we seep into a shameful state of being.

The choice of perceiving any moment in love or fear will be the number one indicator of how you experience this journey you are experiencing here on Planet Earth.

If you believe you must do something, become something, or acquire something else outside of yourself, you will most likely have a chaotic ride at times. Fear will tell you that you need something more to find what you are seeking. And that is not true.

The truth is that you are on a journey of unlearning fear and remembering love.

The closer you get to discovering love in every situation, the more joy and happiness and satisfaction you will experience with everything you encounter. As we discover the true love that resides within us, we find more satisfaction with relationships because our happiness doesn't depend on this relationship. We can detach ourselves from the other person if they are having a bad day because their having a bad day doesn't mean we have to have one too. We can love the car or the house or the toys we purchase because they are one more thing to enjoy in our experience, but if they went away tomorrow, that feeling of inner joy and peace would remain present.

So where did I start and where might you consider starting?

Start at the beginning.

Reintroduce yourself to yourself. Learn to be curious instead of holding disdain for yourself as an individual. Start to pick up on the subtle cues of your heart and how your intuition works. This book will be a great resource for you to learn the skills, and then I can hold your hand along the way, but it is you who will be tuning in. I can't read or hear your personal messages. I can pick up on your energy, but I don't have the ability to tell you exactly how you will receive this.

You will need to practice the skills of learning how to hear and take action on intuition. This is one of the greatest gifts you will ever receive because you will no longer need to go on an endless search in order to find out what the answer is. You will simply turn within. You may be relearning this, or perhaps you will be discovering it for the first time. But you DO have intuition; you simply have forgotten and disconnected from yourself.

Intuition is really learning to live life through your heart instead of your mind. You may have heard someone say, "get out of your head and into your heart."

What does that mean anyway?

It means that we go to our heart space when we have questions, when we need to feel more peace, want to experience more love, and want to connect with others. It is where we find a source of "knowing" rather than an endless loop of thoughts, trying to figure things out.

To understand this shift I think of a quote that my dear friend Laurel Huston says: "If our head is a clock and our heart is a compass . . . why do we ask a clock for directions?"

When we use our head for answers, we tend to feel confused and tired, and we have no energy.

I used to spend a lot of time in my head thinking about everything. I have the 11s on my forehead to prove it. I dissected and analyzed everything in my life, and if I am honest with myself, I still fall into that pattern from time to time because it was how I lived my life for so many years.

You'll know you are using your head to make decisions when the old pros and cons list comes out. Our brain will want to know what is next, what to expect, and how to prepare for the future. And that is okay because our mind is purposeful. It keeps us safe while we are in our human form. It analyzes data to ensure we are going to survive. We can love it, but it doesn't get to run the show. However, when we let it run the show, it is like a crazy, drugged-up bus driver is trying to frantically call the shots and bringing a busload of thoughts along with it.

As much as your mind would like for you to think it is you, you are not your mind. You are not the crazy monkey inside of you that can't keep focused and runs around and jumps from thought to thought. You are not the voice that ensures that you see the possible what ifs in life that might pose a future problem. You are not the mentally unstable version of yourself. It is simply your ego trying to convince you that it needs to be the one making decisions because it is the "stable one." In this space you will feel overwhelmed, frustrated, anxious, and nervous.

And tired. Using the head space continually will lead you to feel absolutely zapped for energy. It takes an enormous amount of energy to continually listen to that voice inside of your head. And it is exhausting.

Once you see your mind for what it is, you can become the observer and allow it to go on its crazy sprees. Then you can make a conscious decision to either lean into that fear that your mind is bringing up inside, or to lean into love and the heart space that allows the real version to take front and center.

I like to stop the madness by breathing in, holding it, and consciously dropping into my heart. The intention is all that you need. Many use meditation in order to get there, and that is a fantastic place to start. Meditation is a practice that is non-negotiable for starting and ending my days. It clears my mind and allows me to drop into that heart space easily. So simply breathing and setting an intention to open my heart space is natural. And you will find that this is actually the most natural thing we can do; we simply have forgotten.

When you drop into your heart for answers, or for clarity, peace, or love, you will have all of the energy you want or need. Life Source Energy resides in that space and connects you directly to the Divine. You may call it anything you desire. I find peace in using the words God, and Jesus Christ, and Spirit, but you may call it the name that feels right to you. It is all the same thing. So as I write those words in this book, simply swap out the word of your choosing and don't let it distract you from learning the principles.

The answers in our heart will always be associated with love. It has no other choice. Love will take the mask of blindness off of you and you will start to see things differently. It will no longer be important to be right about anything. Your relationships will change because you meet them with love instead of fear. Fear always creates division and separation. Love brings cohesion and compassion.

This whole book is based on this. Truth resides in love. Truth never changes.

So keep reading and let's continue learning together.

The next principle requires some muscle, action, and courage.

You need to take out the old garbage—the emotional residue—that you haven't been able or were unwilling to process in the moment you experienced it. This energy may have been trapped inside of you for quite some time, blocking your heart from being fully open to receive all of the energy, vitality, and love you can experience.

Every human on earth has experienced some type of trauma at some point in their lives. It is simply a fact. The way an individual has experienced their life and interpreted their experiences often influences the meaning that individual assigns to their trauma. Particularly sensitive individuals may form multiple meanings around their trauma. They form a story around something that happens and this story allows them to hang onto the emotions, instead of letting those emotions flow through them. Even a particularly resilient person will have opportunities to hang onto things. If you bring up an event in your life and can still feel the sorrow, or the embarrassment, or the emotion behind that event, you have chosen to hang onto the emotion.

These emotions build up and block you from feeling pure joy, pure love, and pure peace.

So it is absolutely necessary to release these emotions in order to live a truth-based existence where you are living from your own inner space of love rather than relying on anything outside of yourself.

The last step is putting on a new pair of glasses so you can see the world differently. The world doesn't need to change externally; you simply need to see it with new eyes. This process takes your current stories, beliefs, and programs and places them out in the open to view them in the light. Anything left in the dark decays. Bringing your stories, beliefs, and programs into the light will help you to see them clearly. When you see them clearly for the first time, most will be exposed as the lies they have always been, and you will be able to have compassion for those who have been exposed to those lies.

This step will take you away from the ego, and the ego's perception, and back into your heart where you can see things clearly with new eyes and a new way of being. And as Meggan Watterson says, "We are here to let our ideas go up in flames, so that beneath the ashes, the soft core of who we truly are arises. And so that we remember that it's not the heart that ever breaks; it's the ego. The heart only ever expands."

These steps are going to challenge you. They require you to do things differently than you have in the past. Many will trigger deep feelings within you, and if they do . . . welcome them. Triggers are simply a sign that you are exposing something in yourself that you have the opportunity to work on. And what a beautiful gift and opportunity that is.

But I can promise you one thing—you will find the answers you have always been searching for. You will undoubtedly find peace, love, joy, and connection.

You will find them because they never left you; you simply need to gently shake yourself awake to discover them. They are with you, because they are within each and every one of us. We are pure love coming from the highest order of compassion and love. We are one with that energy, and it is simply the stories, shame, and fear that blind us from seeing them.

Once you see, you cannot unsee. And it is beautiful and magnificent to behold.

Points to Ponder:

- Start noticing fear and love in action. Your body will help you understand what you are experiencing. If you are feeling constricted, stressed, anxious, and tight, you are leaning into fear. If you feel light, expansive, open, and peaceful, you are leaning into love. Simply notice and observe. At the beginning you may not know how to get out of that space, but you will learn.

- When making decisions, watch for the signs that show whether you are using your mind or your heart. Are you tensing up your forehead and squinting your eyes? You most likely are trying to "figure things out." Simply pause and breathe and set an intention to drop down into your heart. What comes up for you? Keep a journal to jot down your impressions. Be compassionate in these first exercises. You don't need to change anything yet—simply notice.

Chapter 3
TRUTH ABOUT THE BODY

"No! Stop! Make it stop! He isn't supposed to be born yet!!" I screamed at the doctor who had met me in that cold room in the hospital emergency room.

"Calm down, ma'am. He isn't going to survive. You need to push," he said.

I couldn't even wrap my brain around this. My water had broken at nineteen weeks and I had thought they would simply put me on bed rest for the remainder of my pregnancy.

And here the doctor was making me push. I knew in my heart if the baby was born, he wouldn't survive and I would not be going home with my baby in my arms.

And then it hit me . . . I wouldn't be going home with a baby in my arms.

When Cole, my baby, was born, his spinal cord wasn't fully developed. He wouldn't have survived even at full term.

And I was crushed.

My sister had lost her twin babies the month before, and I was still recovering from the deep grief I felt for her. I had felt guilty for being pregnant with Cole because I had already been pregnant twice before and had borne those two amazing children (and I hadn't "planned" those pregnancies) and here was my uber responsible sister who was having a hard time even having one child.

And now I was grieving my baby that wouldn't be raised in my family unit. I wasn't even allowed to bury him because they were going to test him to find out what had happened.

But I already knew what had happened.

My husband had tried every supplement and pharmaceutical on the market for a skin rash that looked similar to acne. This condition started when he was working out in the oil fields and was exposed to some toxic chemicals.

The only solution the doctors had was to put more toxic chemicals inside of him. When all other prescriptions he had tried were ineffective, they encouraged him to take a drug called Accutane. This was a wonder drug for all things related to skin issues . . . or so they said. They did mention the side effects; and on the package of Accutane it clearly stated that it would promote birth defects in babies. After a thorough discussion with the dermatologist, my husband felt very secure that there were no risks involved in our future baby's health, because they said birth defects only occurred when the mother took the drug, not when the dad took it.

But here was my lifeless baby boy, lying on a surgical tray with a severed spine—just like the picture on the Accutane box.

And I was mad as hell.

There isn't a force in nature that can hold back a mad mama bear's heart from forging forward to find a solution for the madness that impacts a child. So I called the doctor, I called the pharmacist, and I called the drug company.

And no one would answer my calls. They were too afraid of the liability. And they couldn't face the possibility that their research, or lack of research, had failed them in ensuring the safety of the humans they were feeding it to.

After a while, I realized that they weren't going to listen, and that they were more interested in the almighty dollar than the impact they would have on the world. And I realized that the only thing I could control was my future decisions for my body. I needed to listen to my body, instead of everyone else around me, because it was 100% *my* responsibility—not theirs. It was time to take back my power for my health, my body, and my spirit and bring them back into one holistic being.

And that is when things started to shift for me. I started to realize that I needed to listen and be intuitive to what my body needed, instead of allowing others to dictate my journey. The world will tell you that *it* is the only source of knowledge and that we need to leave everything to the professionals that have been medically trained.

Even though I was on an anti-doctor kick for a while, I have navigated back to a place where I know it is important to take advantage of new testing methods *and* to listen to my heart. My heart leads me to find the right treatment, the right protocol, and the right person that will work in partnership with me and allow me to keep my voice and empower me to take control of my health and body. The keyword here is "partnership," and I am in charge of the final decision, because I have the answers inside; I only need to listen and take action.

When did we give away all of our power over our bodies?

When did we start listening to everyone else instead of our own intuitive abilities to help us navigate ways to show up and help our bodies heal?

When did we stop trusting that our bodies could heal on their own if we are compassionate and loving and ready to hear what they have to say?

I boldly proclaim that the powers at work knew that if they cut us off from our bodies, we wouldn't understand how to receive our intuition and the "knowing" that we are all born with. If we aren't aligned with our bodies, chances are great that we aren't fully aligned with Source Energy at all times either, and thus we don't have the full power to navigate this lifetime with grace and ease.

The world powers have understood that their greatest advantage in the power play is to convince us that our bodies are our enemies—that we will never measure up to the world standards of what is acceptable, and beautiful, and desirable. The "world" also programmed us to believe that we can't hear what our bodies have to say, and that we need to rely on all of the Western medicine techniques and pharmaceuticals to help us stop feeling.

Because heaven forbid we actually *feel* something.

As a collective, we don't want to feel. We want to numb, avoid, distract, and do anything but feel.

So we gave away our power over our bodies to everyone else. We gave it to those that would tell us how to look, how to eat, and how to make it all turn off.

It is ironic that feeling is what we came down to Earth for—to experience our bodies and to experience emotions. The only thing different from the next world and this one is that we get to experience bodies and emotions.

So why do we choose to turn it off all of the time? Why are we at war with the thing that should be our greatest teammate in this lifetime?

Our bodies that can help guide us back to our hearts, where we can feel good again?

The one thing we are all searching for is to feel good again.

But how do we do that if the very vehicle that can get us there is spit upon and looked down upon with disgust every day? The reality is, if we will learn to forgive and become compassionate and loving with this vessel of truth, we will find what we are searching for because our vessel will guide us there.

Our bodies can be used as a GPS in this lifetime, to help us get back on track, to help us understand our emotions, and to allow us to feel, with all five senses, the wonderful world in which we live.

Imagine a world in which we experience love through everything we touch, see, hear, smell, and taste. This is the world we can all have if we choose to stop leaning into the fear that embraces body hatred, and lean into love, which allows us to have compassion and connection to our bodies.

It sounds easy, but it may take some of us a lifetime to get back to that state of oneness. Our stories and trauma and programming will need to be removed layer by layer in order to expose our heart center fully. This center is where we can connect to everything around us in that space of love.

However . . . trauma blocks that flow.

The definition of trauma is "a deeply distressing or disturbing experience." I am pretty confident that each person reading this can identify with that passage. Many traumas were experienced as children, because as children, we couldn't put things into proper perspective. Even if your mother left you at daycare when you were young and you didn't understand what was happening, you experienced some trauma. We will all experience some trauma in our lives.

In addition, many individuals have a trauma story around their bodies, which can cause them to become detached, distrustful, and even mortified at the sight of their bodies. Bodies have become the enemy and we are taught to try to change them on a regular basis. There are very few individuals in this world who truly love their bodies, and so the majority may, and most likely do, have a trauma story around them.

Add to this that most of us have experienced sexual trauma (yes, I am being bold with that statement), and have a recipe for disconnection. I am being bold because perhaps not everyone has been raped or molested, but how many of us have had sex when we wanted to say no, or have said "no" to a spouse and they insisted on having it anyway? How many of us have had "duty" sex?

This is trauma and it has been stored as such. It may not be as deeply ingrained as it is in a person who has been through extensive sexual trauma, but it is trauma, nonetheless.

And trauma disconnects us with our bodies. Many sexual trauma victims get so good at disconnecting that they literally disassociated from themselves in the moment that they were victimized. It is not unheard of for someone to recall their story much later in life as they start to feel safe and their bodies allow for this new awareness to unfold once again.

It would make sense that between the world telling us that we are not enough and that our bodies are flawed, and the disconnection we experience from trauma, we would need to relearn how to connect with our bodies once again.

It's time my friends. It is time to collectively heal together. I am sure you have felt the changes in the air. There are things that have never happened before in the history of the world, and we are right in the middle of it.

We are being urged to heal, and to unify body, mind, and spirit, and to be courageous enough to look at our shadows in order to find the light once again.

And we can do it. *You* can do it.

And on the other side, you will discover that it is worth it. On the other side, we will have a cohesive relationship with our bodies that will help us to discover our intuitive abilities, help us identify our thoughts, and help us make a conscious choice to step out of our stories and into something more loving. And then we can release trauma so that our heart center can be exposed along with a more vibrant and healthy body—a body free of the trauma that weighed it down for so many years.

And you will glow from within. You will fall head over heels in love with this amazing partner in life and you will start to shift into a new paradigm and have a new perspective in life.

It's not to say you won't have challenges or days that feel more difficult—you and I are human and this is the human experience—but you can have peace, even amid the chaos. You can find purpose in every moment you experience, if you choose to.

So what is next? "Where is a good place to start?" you may ask.

Let's start with the place we disconnected first—our bodies.

This is where we start. We start by forming an alliance with one of our greatest enemies.

In order to learn the truth about intuition, meditation, releasing trauma, and discovering the power of emotions, it is important to start with feeling safe in our bodies and get ourselves into a state of calm and peace, instead of fight and flight. I find that it is helpful to classify three intentions:

- Safety
- Connecting back into our body (which we will discuss throughout the book)
- Creating a strong and balanced nervous system (I will teach you several tools to help you in future chapters)

Safety. It is first on the list. I can imagine that some of you are thinking to yourselves: "I feel safe. Why is that the first one on the list?"

In response, I would encourage you to consider that perhaps there is a chance that you don't actually feel safe, and that your actions speak louder than your understanding. Most of us don't feel safe and we choose our favorite mechanism for handling that fear. I am certain you have heard "fight or flight," which is the amygdala's response to threats. The root problem is that we live in a world where we perceive things as a constant threat. We are always "on" and never turn it off for a second. Or we turn it off completely and shut down because it is too much to handle any of it.

Consider these four areas of trauma responses and see if you fit into one category more than another.

- Flight: workaholic, overthinker, anxiety, panic, can't sit still, perfectionist
- Fight: controlling, "the bully," narcissist, angry outbursts, explosive behavior
- Freeze: difficulty making decisions, feeling stuck, dissociating, isolating, numb
- Fawn: people pleaser, lack of identity, no boundaries, overwhelmed, codependent, attachment

You may find more than one category that you filter back and forth through; mine tended to be flight and fawn. I would keep myself so busy that I didn't have time to think about anything. By playing the game of avoiding, numbing, and escaping, I became a master at avoiding everything hard in my life. That was my go-to in my business and career world. When I was around my family, I would immediately go into fawn to try to make everyone feel included and happy. I would dance around the family unit trying to ensure that the happiness meter was high and that we were all getting along and singing "Kumbaya." I made decisions only after asking each person what they would like to do and giving them ten choices if they didn't offer an idea. It was an energy sucking way to live. I remember one day my very vocal daughter threw up her hands in the air and said, "Mom, just make a freakin' decision! Why do you constantly try to make everyone happy? It just pisses us all off!"

Yep, our families are our greatest teachers. This feisty little five-foot-nothing girl has taught me more lessons than I can share in this book. I remember feeling very offended in the moment, but as I looked at what she said, I realized she was exactly right. I wasn't helping by trying to tiptoe around every family member to make sure they were okay. I needed to make sure *I* was okay and then everyone around me would settle into the decisions I made based on that.

In fact, most trauma responses can be used as a mirror to our souls. In my fawn state, I was desperately seeking someone to help me feel okay because I most certainly did NOT feel okay. The ironic thing is that the person I needed most was me. *I* was the one who had left many years ago, and now it was time to reunify with that scared and lonely version of Wendy.

I now understand that when I tune in with myself, consider what I want and need, and step out of self-betrayal, I can indeed feel "okay." This state of okayness invites others to feel okay as well. They can either choose to come along for the ride or choose something different, and even if they aren't "okay," it is understood that this is the way of life and they are in the midst of learning. It is my job to stay out of their lane.

No regret, no stress, no guilt—just living life the way it should be lived.

A trauma response happens when we don't feel safe.

So feeling safe, getting back into our bodies, and then turning down the knob on our response to stress is crucial to feeling a sense of wellness and peace. Inner peace and spirituality are challenging when we can't think, or focus, or feel *and* we have extreme fatigue.

I once heard a great teacher say, "Until you get the body chemistry right, you can't work with the spirit."

Makes sense.

So now that you are aware of what your trauma responses are, it is time to do something about it. We often hold a belief that most people live in their trauma responses, so it's just the way we have to live our lives. But life isn't meant to be lived this way. We are not meant to live this way. We are meant to have peace, moments of pause and reflection, experiences in giving and receiving love and compassion, and feelings of pleasure.

Most of the chapters in this book are dedicated to the truths I have found that have helped me to feel safe, come back to my body, and regulate my nervous system. I believe that God knew that I couldn't live my personal truth with the blinders that this fear was placing on my eyes. It was time to release the lies and the insanity I had instilled into my life.

The truths that have helped me are threaded throughout this book to help you in your intention to heal. Those healing truths can't be contained in just one chapter because we have a lifetime of thoughts, actions, and programming that have brought us to where we are with our bodies today.

But we will start in this chapter with reviewing the very basic needs we can meet in order to help us move into that feeling of safety. Let's start with the lowest level of Maslow's Hierarchy of Needs: the basic physiological necessities of food, water, rest, air, and reproduction.

If you don't feed your body or give it water, you won't feel safe. But how many of us plow our way through the day and forget to eat? We feel the urge to go to the bathroom during a meeting and we won't allow ourselves to go and relieve ourselves. It is imperative to do the small things in life in order to help our bodies know they can trust us.

Taking the small step in feeding our bodies, ensuring that we aren't thirsty, and relieving ourselves seems basic, but we self-betray all of the time. Start with taking care of the basics.

After you get the hang of simply eating, then start to choose your food wisely. As with everything, food has energetic properties and if you want to feel vibrant, alert, and passionate in life, you would be smart to eat foods that will feed and nourish, instead of deplete, your body. I don't believe I even need to go into detail about these foods; you intuitively know that what is grown here on the earth is more vibrant than dead or non-living food on the shelf.

So start there.

Then you can add in some very easy techniques to continue in your safety plan. These action items are so simple that you can do them while doing your normal life activities. They won't add anything to your routine, and you will most likely find that you can do it more easily and with more flow and less stress.

Next we focus on breath. I told you these are simple.

The only autonomic response we can control is breathing. God gave us everything we need to thrive on this earth, and breathing can transform your life if you remember and learn how to do it properly. I have written an entire chapter dedicated to breath . . . it is that important, and most of us don't breathe correctly. We breathe from our chest instead of from our belly—that is how we breathe when we are running—and that tells our bodies that we need to prepare for flight. So right now, as you read this chapter, consider starting to breathe correctly. Breathe into and out of your abdomen instead of through the chest. The only thing you need to do in order to breathe this way is to focus your intention on it and it will happen naturally.

Another simple technique is grounding, which is basically touching the earth's energy with our feet and/or our body.

We typically have rubber under our feet and so even though we are walking around much of the day, we don't actually feel the earth. There is an energetic connection between the earth and us, and simply going out and feeling the earth under our feet has an amazing calming effect on both our bodies and our minds. When you let Mother Earth envelop you in Her comfort and support, you will feel amazingly calm and clear after stepping on Her. It is an incredible practice to step out onto grass first thing in the morning when the sun is first up. This practice also will help you sleep better as it helps your natural circadian rhythm become more balanced.

These practices are so easy, and yet so powerful. As you start feeling safe again, you will most likely start feeling better about yourself and your body. You will start feeling less anxiety and more peace.

When you do this, you are ready to start listening to your body and stop being reactive when it speaks to you. Then you can start hearing and understanding the messages more clearly. It will be like you have turned the dial on the stereo ever so slightly until the reception becomes crystal clear and you can start having a conversation with your body, instead of listening to a toddler having a tantrum. And just like a toddler, you need to help your body feel safe before you can hear what it is saying and why it is saying that.

This entire book is dedicated to helping you to learn the language of your body, mind, and spirit. Most of the practices I share will help you start to lower your stress level and allow your nervous system to come back into balance. Your cortisol level will reduce and you will sleep better, stop reacting so easily to outside stimuli, and feel a sense of peace and well-being.

And when your internal world starts to shift, you will see that shift transfer to your external world.

Many people, when they feel safe, will experience excess weight start to simply fall off because our bodies don't need that extra protection anymore. As we gain more love, we increase our confidence quotient and financial abundance shows up more easily and almost effortlessly. And the relationships in our lives are strengthened and begin to shift into healthier bonds.

Here is where we start: with the basics.

Points to Ponder:

- Listen to the basic responses your body is sending you and honor those responses by showing up. Feed your body when it is hungry, drink water throughout the day, and relieve yourself when you need to go to the bathroom. Crazy simple, right? It's even crazier that most of us have developed habits that go against these basic principles of safety and health.

- Breathe from your belly instead of your chest. Notice a few times during the day where you are breathing and if it is in your chest, be intentional and drop it down to your belly. This will help your nervous system to know you are safe and to stop hyper-reacting.

- Do a simple grounding practice each day. When you wake up in the morning, go outside and feel the earth under your feet, close your eyes, and turn your face up toward the morning sunlight. This simple practice will help you to get back your body and will allow you to receive the energy from the earth.

- Discover a full practice of powerful techniques and understanding through my online course, "Now…let's heal." This is a comprehensive course on getting you back into safety and into your body, and turning down the "flight/fight" response in your body. Go to http://wendybunnell.com for more information.

Chapter 4
TRUTH ABOUT INTUITION

The text notification on my phone went off again. I was about to chuck the dang thing at the wall.

I felt trapped. I was like a caged animal that couldn't escape the confines of the career I had chosen for the past eight years.

I had done everything possible to line things up for the next five days. I dotted every "i" and crossed every "t" so that I could go to this couple's retreat and be present with my lover.

And yet . . . the phone kept ringing.

Deadlines that never go away, and real estate clients that have legitimate concerns for the biggest purchase they will likely make in their lifetime . . . and yet all I desired was quiet for a moment.

And the anger and frustration set in. I finally allowed those emotions to fill me up from the corners of my heart, where I had nicely stuffed them away. I should know by now that they don't stay forever in that space and they will fester and grow to a place in which I will eventually be forced to see and observe the mess I wasn't willing to clean up when it was more manageable.

But this was the way I put bread on the table. How could I simply run away from a half million-dollar business?

I had pretended that I could simply train others and take a part-time role in my business, but it wasn't working.

My heart kept pleading with me to consider leaving this industry, but my head was at war with my heart and kept telling it to shut up and suck it up.

We gathered in a circle of couples toward the end of the retreat and my body felt like it was on fire from the anger that was erupting.

The facilitator encouraged us to bring up anything that needed to be brought out to the light. She encouraged us to realize that everything mattered to this relationship, and that if one area of our life was out of balance, it would impact every other area as well.

I stood up and exclaimed, "I have stayed in an industry that has slowly sucked the life out of me! My heart has been asking me to be courageous for years, and I keep pretending not to hear it, and today I am choosing to stop self-betraying and listen!"

The facilitator lovingly asked, "What does it say, my friend?"

I explained that I had spent eight years accumulating wealth and material things; that I loved the industry for teaching me abundance and the laws of money and receiving; and that, while I looked around my home with a heart of gratitude and love, I wondered why I still felt so unfulfilled.

"I am recognizing that I am not using my spiritual gifts: my gift of communication, my gift of gathering and loving others, my gift of courage. I have been stuffing them away because the last time I opened them up, they almost cost me my life.

"I am so scared of showing up to be seen that I am slowly dying because I am unwilling to face my fears," I said shakily.

"So, what does your heart tell you that you should do?" she asked lovingly.

"I am done. I am retiring and I am ready to sacrifice, if necessary, but my soul is more important than any monetary means, any home, any car, any trinket. I am choosing me." I breathed in and received and then said in a bold declaration of love, "I choose me!!"

And absolute joy and peace set in.

Listening to your heart isn't always the easy route on a cognizant level. Your mind will try to talk you out of it. Every.Single.Time.

On the flip side, it is always liberating as we expand and become the person we desire to express.

But, that also doesn't mean it isn't scary as hell after we choose it.

That night, my husband tossed and turned with the fear that was tearing him apart after realizing that I was leaving the comfort and ease of the money flow and choosing the unknown. As we lay there clinging to each other, I asked him to breathe, to receive confirmation that all would be well.

He started to relax and together, we talked about the positive "what ifs" instead of the negative "what ifs" that we were both considering.

And the fact is, we both know that miracles happen every single time we choose to listen to our hearts instead of our minds.

Every.Single.Time.

But for many, listening to intuition is not easy. The world has programmed us to listen to everyone *but* our own intuition and our own hearts. From a young age, we are told "no" more times than "yes," we are told to listen to our elders and to our teachers, and to stuff down our natural tendencies and desires to conform to the rules of life.

It is now time to return to that place of all-knowing and love.

It is time to rediscover your truth.

The number one question I get asked is, "How do I hear answers, and how do I learn to trust my intuition?" They ask because the world has become increasingly noisy. They can't hear anymore. For so long, they have been *told* where to seek answers that at this point, they have forgotten how to hear that inner voice.

So, this is where we start to understand the language of our hearts.

How do we hear that voice? you may ask.

Honestly, I can't answer that question perfectly for you, because we all hear it slightly differently. Some of you are visual learners, others auditory, and many others are kinesthetic and tactile learners. So, the way you receive and perceive messages is going to be unique to your own DNA coding.

I invite you to think back to a time when you were young—a time before the world had programmed you—and remember a time when you heard or felt something that invoked a sense of "knowing."

I can recall my first remembrance of hearing the Divine, when I was just a young girl.

The year was 1975 and it was a fabulous year to be five years old. Tack on the fact that I lived in California, had access to a pool in my backyard, the ocean less than an hour away, and Disneyland "around the corner," and I felt like the luckiest girl alive.

On a beautiful California day, my family and friends all piled into the old faithful station wagon to go to Disneyland for the day. These were the "old" days, according to my kids, when seat belts weren't even on our radar. I shared the very back with three other kids and we hunkered down for the ninety-minute trek.

Disney never gets old for me. There is something magical in the park, where thousands of creative geniuses have come together to take us into another world, another land, evoking a new feeling around every corner. As a visionary leader, I can appreciate and stare in wonder and awe each time I visit.

As the park started to close, the crew started to head toward the gate. My father and I walked hand in hand down Main Street, stopping several times to look at the window displays in several of the shops. Toward the end, there was a beautiful, miniature rendition of the Sleeping Beauty Castle. We stopped once again and I was mesmerized by the miniature version of the large castle that was just up the street.

When I looked up, my dad wasn't there anymore.

I ran toward what I thought was my dad, but when I looked up, it wasn't him. I didn't realize how many people have dark brown-black hair until that moment. It seemed as though there was a sea of men that all looked exactly like my father.

After what seemed like an eternity, I felt myself being tugged toward a bench at the front of the park. I sat down and remembered, word for word, a story that was told at church. The story was about a little boy who got lost in the woods and heard a voice telling him to stay there and not to go in search of his family, but to let his family come to him.

God was indeed speaking to me in the language of my learning. I understood stories and words, and so I wrapped my arms around my knees and cried softly as I sat on that bench. The words, "Stay put. Don't go find your family. Let your family come and find you" were received in my heart.

Moments later, a kind woman approached me and asked if I was lost. I told her, "I am not lost, but I can't find my mommy and daddy." This statement makes me laugh because Disneyland is my stomping ground and I *did* know exactly where I was; I simply didn't know where my family was.

She took me to the lost-and-found across the street, and I was immediately met by very kind cast members who then went in search of my family. In 1975, there were no easy ways to communicate, and I didn't know anything other than my first name and that my mom's name was Joan and my dad's name was Joe.

I heard them broadcasting over the speaker, "If you are missing a lost little girl, please come to the lost and found." I saw the concern start to show in their faces with each page that went unanswered. I am sure they didn't have a protocol back then as to what to do with a child that was left by her parents.

After what seemed like forever, my father walked into the building and started crying. I don't think I had ever seen my father cry before. I responded with anger. I was mad! Why did he leave me? I was scared and confused and I didn't understand why he would leave me there for so long. After some time, my body softened and I cried tears of joy that I felt safe once again in the arms of my father, who did indeed come back for me.

I later learned that my family had all loaded up in the station wagon and had headed toward our home. They got on the freeway toward Ventura County. On the way home, my brother decided he wanted to see his little sister squirm after eating some red-hot candy he had. He called my name out several times and when he didn't see me, he said, "Mom, where is Wendy?"

She said, "Kyle, that's not even funny, She is in the back of the car." Of course, they quickly discovered that this was not the case and crossed over the median to get back on the opposite side of the freeway to come and rescue me.

Yep, I was the child that got lost and left at Disneyland. As a parent, I can understand the sheer panic it must have created for my mom and dad. However, as with every single major moment in my life, I have learned some pivotal shifts in my understanding.

I heard something. I heard a voice and saw pictures come to life in my mind. Even at the young age of five, I knew that those thoughts and that story weren't my own thoughts; there was something larger than myself guiding me, holding my hand, and helping me along this journey.

While it has taken me decades to know that the power of that *force* is with me in every moment, and that I have access anytime I want, I have never doubted that this *spirit* is with me always.

I shut the door to hearing this voice for a while when the world was more important than the voice—when the need to be included and accepted overtook the importance of showing up authentically. So many of us go through this phase around our teenage years as we try to get attention from that cute boy or girl in class, when we try to fit in with the "cool kids," or hope to make the cut for the drill team. Noise starts to overtake us and we get busy—very busy—with all the "important" things, and never leave room to hear.

I spent my teen years and my twenties being tossed about and in the depth of misery because I felt like I simply couldn't get life right—that there was something innately flawed by my existence—and so I kept choosing things that would bring me suffering and pain. And in my mind, I deserved it.

I am certain my spirit was trying desperately to help me, but couldn't get through because the reception was too fuzzy. It was as if my dial on the radio was slightly off the station and I could only hear static. And just like the radio, all I needed to do was to barely change the dial by not even a fraction of an inch to start hearing again.

And like a muscle that hasn't been used for a while, our reception gets weak. Many don't believe there is an inner voice at all, while others feel that they need to do something in order to receive it; if only I fasted more, prayed more, performed the religious rituals of my faith more, served more, did more.

You realize this concept is absurd once you are on the other side, because the doing in our lives is drowning out the being. We are left feeling exhausted, defeated, and" less than" every single time we justify the reason we aren't hearing this Source Energy.

You can't "do" yourself to remembering. You simply need to "be" in order to feel that beautiful peace, joy, and knowingness that only comes from aligning with truth.

So just like you wouldn't rush to the gym and start lifting 200-pound weights to get your muscles in shape (that would be foolish), but rather start with lower weights and gradually work up to higher weights, you start smaller with exercising the intuition muscle. You help your subconscious understand that it is safe for you to trust once again by beginning with the things you feel aren't as important.

A dear friend asked me about discovering the power of intuition and making decisions with a heart-centered approach, and I gave him this same advice. I said, "Start with listening to the gentle pull of your heart as you simply live, and then take action on those small things, and watch what unfolds."

He called me a couple weeks later, and I could feel the beam on his face as he spoke—joy is something you can feel, even if you're not in the same room.

"Wendy, I took action on a small step the other day, and I wanted to share it with you!" he exclaimed.

My friend told me about a family member who was suffering from a chronic illness and had some heavy burdens placed upon him. The rest of the family took the approach of staying positive and giving him space to process, but when my friend saw this family member, he could feel the weight his family member was carrying. That inner voice began gently nudging my friend to ask his family member how he really was. That question brought the floodgates of emotion and a sense of relief to that young man because my friend gave him permission to feel, to be heard, and to possibly be understood.

What a loving connection that probably was for my friend. He showed up in love and as a result, both of them felt the power of Source in both of their lives. The simple process of feeling, or hearing, or getting the impression to do something, and then taking action, is what will start this process for you.

My amazing friend and mentor, Laurel Huston, calls it "tuning in and turning on."

It's the process of recognizing that peaceful direction and using your free agency to take action.

And each time you use intuition, you come away with a sense of awe for the miracle that has just appeared in your life, even in those small moments. *A Course in Miracles* states, "Miracles occur naturally as expressions of love. The real miracle is the love that inspires them. In this sense, everything that comes from love is a miracle."

Tuning in can be much more effective if you use some tried and true tools. Prayer is my favorite tool. Call upon whatever source resonates with you (because honestly, they are all the same source, simply using different names). Prayer utilizes the power of faith, trust, words, and intention to bring magical results. Asking for direction, help, comfort, and peace will help you to start understanding the language of your heart. We will be doing a deep dive into prayer, but for now, you can start practicing whatever prayer method works best for you.

It is important to know that you do not need to pray in a certain way. I know that when I kneel down and fold my arms, my mind wanders and I start getting cold and my back starts aching. This method doesn't work for me, and others have mentioned their challenge in praying in this "traditional" manner. I have a highly active mind and so I find that praying while washing dishes, hiking, driving, or meditating seems to work best for me.

Understand this: you can't mess this up. It isn't possible. God is always with you, as it is inside of you; you simply need to learn how to open the door to understand and receive answers.

As you progress and start using prayer for big decisions, you may find that signs can be very helpful in order for you to start trusting your intuition.

I discovered this trick after reading some of Gabby Bernstein's books. She uses this technique to ensure she is on the right track.

I love this method for any major decision I have on my journey, and it is absolutely amazing and jaw dropping each time it happens. In fact, I usually will start laughing from my core each time it unfolds. It is absolutely magical to me.

The first time I tried praying about a major decision was about four years ago. My husband was about to retire and we were excited to move to our dream destination and plant roots in what we consider paradise. I love the desert, the red rock, and the opportunity to be outside without a jacket almost all year round. The sun is in the same category as food and water so this was my ticket to having it shine upon me 325 days per year.

It was apparent that I needed to change real estate brokerages because the one I was working for at the time didn't have a branch in southern Utah. My broker encouraged me to open a new office, but I felt that in my health condition at that time, it would simply be too much pressure to put on my healing body.

So, I started interviewing. I met with two brokers in the town I was moving to, and not only didn't feel right about either one, but had anxiety at the interviews. As a side note, our bodies will give us messages; we just need to listen. My body was expressing a disconnect in those meetings—that our missions didn't align and I needed to keep looking.

My cousin worked at a brokerage four hours away from where I was relocating and had asked me a couple of times to simply meet with her broker before I made the final decision. As I stepped into that office, something shifted in my body, sending me waves of calmness and peace. I don't even remember what the interviewer said, but I can remember vividly what I felt.

Now in my more seasoned stage of accessing intuition, I would spot that feeling and realize that was my answer. However, this was a huge decision for us and since I would be the breadwinner for the whole family when we move, it was a very important decision to get right.

I sat in prayer that evening and asked God to show me a large yellow and black butterfly in the next 24 hours if this was the best option for me to take. I made the decision in my mind that if I didn't see one, I would continue my search, and if I did see one, I would take bold action and sign with a brokerage that didn't make any logical sense at all for me to join.

After waking up the next morning, I put this thought out of my mind and went about my day. I got busy with work, and while I was talking to a client in my backyard (my office), I was in the middle of a sentence when a movement caught my eye. Heading in my direction was a large black and yellow butterfly. It flew slowly enough that I could watch it fly gracefully in front of me, ensuring that I would take note of it.

Tears sprang to my eyes. Not only did I receive this message that would change my whole career, but the mere fact that my simple question mattered in the grand scheme of life filled me with gratitude and love.

At first this decision came with a lot of resistance. The new brokerage meant taking a "split" once again with a full-service brokerage. I had just left a boutique brokerage where I only had to pay $500 per transaction and would be moving to a split where the brokerage would take a much larger cut of my pay. Nothing about this decision made logical sense. I would pay more to be aligned with them. I would live four hours away, making it virtually impossible for me to go to meetings, get things printed, and get support. Why would my intuition lead me here?

It honestly didn't matter because my heart said, "Go." That visual sign helped me make a very important decision and allowed me to step boldly into it.

The ease of the decision didn't make the next steps come easily, though. For eight months after signing with the new brokerage, I continued living in the small town we had been in because my house wouldn't budge on selling. I saw my commission checks come in with a huge chunk of money missing—money that would have been there had I stayed with the previous brokerage. In one frightful state of mind, I even tried to switch back, but then I was reminded that I had signed a three-year contract.

While feeling slightly defeated, I did eventually sell my home and moved to the hometown of my heart and started getting settled. Shortly after I arrived in my new hometown, I met virtually with my new broker and he guided me through some resources that my new company offered.

This new system allowed me to get company online leads. Since I was the only agent from that brokerage in this town four hours away, I was the only agent receiving them. Basically, my new brokerage started sending me buyers in my area every single day. My desire to be successful in a new town as a new agent was realized very quickly because of the bold action I had taken on a decision that didn't make sense. Two years later, I received an award for my production and the success that I had achieved in this new town. I can honestly say that my success was in huge part due to making the choice that didn't make sense and trusting my inner guidance.

Had I used the traditional method of getting a piece of paper and writing down the pros and cons, I would never have arrived at this decision. Living a heart-led life means getting quiet, listening, being neutral in the outcome, and taking action once the message is received. It means not analyzing that decision in any way, but trusting that your heart is leading you in the direction of your highest and best benefit.

You will find when you listen, tune in and receive, and then take bold action, that you will start trusting the process more and more as you exercise the intuition muscle. It's okay if you don't see a sign at first. It either means that wasn't the best option, or you were attached to the outcome. Truly trusting means that you trust that either choice is okay, and that you are willing to take action, even if it doesn't align with what your conscious mind has figured out.

I use this force to make every decision in my life. I mean, why wouldn't I? This voice allows me to have absolute clarity and confidence in every step I take. I have gotten so good at hearing it because I practice using it every single day and my intuition muscle is strong. I understand exactly what it feels like when I am taking the step in the right direction and when I am choosing something that isn't in my highest and best benefit. And yes, I still sometimes choose that option. Why? Because sometimes the option is like a huge "God dare" and it takes courage to choose the option that is scary, unknown, and unfamiliar. Sometimes it takes several nudges and even a little kick in my butt to get me to listen. I am human, and my humanness is very apparent at times.

This story can be broken down into three things that need to happen in order to get very good at listening to our inner voice. First, you learn how to hear that voice in the personal context that it is shown to you. Second, take immediate action and choose to shut off the doubting voices around you. Third, stand firm in your decision.

I love that the initial story of listening and trusting is from an experience in my childhood. When we are kids, we are in a position to honor and trust ourselves. We haven't yet learned from life *not* to trust ourselves. We are present in our bodies and we are present in our minds, so it is very easy to hear and take action because our programming is just beginning.

I love that the scriptures—and more specifically, Jesus Christ—encourage us to become like a little child. This knowingness is hard-wired into us, so as children we just feel it, hear it, and act upon it. The great news is that we can relearn the art of wonder and awe, the ease in which life exists, and surrender the programming that keeps us stuck and choosing to live a life of constant struggle.

Becoming like a little child means living right now, in the present moment. Becoming like a little child means pausing from time to time. Becoming like a little child means getting curious and observing your body, your surroundings, and your life with acceptance and love.

You will only hear when you can quiet the mind so the soul can speak.

If you hear and understand your soul—your heart space—you will never fear for the answers. You will never fear for what to do next, and you will never be alone on your journey.

Points to Ponder:

- Understand how your body reacts when you hear a "yes" versus when you hear a "no." Try something that is blatantly incorrect versus correct, such as saying that your name is someone else's name rather than your own given name. What does it feel like when you hear truth versus untruth? Try saying "no" over and over and then saying "yes" over and over. Do you feel the difference? One should feel constrictive while the other will feel expansive; one will be confusing while the other one is clarity and peace.

- Try acting on one thing your heart tells you today. If you see someone in a store that you feel inspired to smile at, act and look them in the eye and smile. If you feel impressed to call someone, pick up the phone and dial their number. Even in these small acts you may find miracles come forward. In fact, I would expect that you would see them unfold before you.

Chapter 5
TRUTH ABOUT EMOTION

It was 1AM and I had once again simply lain in bed. Rest would most likely not come my way. I yearned for solace from the constant pain and the fear that accompanied me like a parasite, but I could not find the answers.

It had been two years without sleep. I would have moments of rest for five to fifteen minutes at a time, but I was weary throughout my entire being.

And this night, all I wanted to do was run. I wanted to run away from my body, away from the pain, away from this life. It was too much; the darkness wandered around with me and I could not see any light—there was simply darkness over my eyes and my heart.

And I felt that it would never end.

So I had to run. I had to get away. I had to get away from this madness that was pervading my soul.

My common sense kicked in and reminded me that if I ran on the road, I would most likely be stopped by a police officer who might take me away and stuff me into a little white rubber room.

So I stepped into my back yard. It wasn't expansive, but it had grass and I needed my bare feet to touch the earth and remind me that I was still alive. And so I ran. I ran in circles over and over and over for what seemed like hours. I ran until my lungs couldn't, and wouldn't, take in breath anymore. I lay down on the grass and looked up at the stars as I regained my breath.

"I am living a nightmare that I can't wake up from . . ." I said out loud.

And I cried. I cried tears of frustration and heartache and pain.

What had I done to deserve this? I thought I was doing so many good things in this world, and yet here I was in never-ending pain and agony.

As I told my coach the following day of my experience, she said to me, "Wendy, you are really good at the Yin, but perhaps you need to experience the Yang. Rather than sitting in stillness and trying to bring in peace, why don't you let out a primal scream and get out the restlessness inside?"

Yes . . . yes! I had never considered screaming or yelling or crying in that manner, because that would be out of control, and a lady must never be out of control. But my soul was ready, and it wasn't going to stay hidden anymore.

So I jumped in the car and drove up to a remote location and pulled off the road.

And I screamed. I screamed until my throat was sore and I had nothing else to give. I screamed at God, and I screamed at my body, and I screamed at Christ. Life was unfair, life was toxic, and life was an effing bad dream.

As I stopped and looked out the windshield, the cloudy, dark sky opened up just ever so slightly, and the rays of the sun shone so brightly into my eyes that I couldn't keep them open any longer.

That was when I saw Him: My Christ. My Brother and Savior. I saw His radiant face and His hands that were open in surrender. And I saw love surrounding every part of His being. He was so bright that I felt my eyes squint, even though they were closed.

"You are ready, Wendy. I never asked you to do this alone."

Solace. Comfort. Hope.

That moment would remain in my heart forever. It was the moment that would carry me through the years to follow that would still challenge me to the very core of my being as I continued to experience my health journey.

In that car I had found a way to let out the pain, even if it was just enough to find a few hours of peace. It became a way to allow the years of trauma, pain, and self-betrayal out of my body, where they had been trapped for years.

I didn't understand at the time why I felt better after I screamed, but I kept doing what was working.

Only later would I understand emotion—energy in motion. And it would all make sense that this emotion was trapped. I hadn't allowed myself to feel, and believed that I was strong enough to simply put everything in the past, so I tucked my emotion nice and tight into the storage of my heart.

I thought it would stay there forever.

But it didn't.

Because I wouldn't wail and scream and feel the things along my journey that I had perceived as trauma, my body would do the job for me.

Emotion. One of the reasons we are on Planet Earth, and yet we run away from emotion over and over thinking we can outrun the energy that is flowing inside of us.

But that is impossible. The energy simply gets stored somewhere until we are brave enough to feel it in order to heal it, or we continue to stuff it down and allow it to build a wall around our hearts.

So we either feel nothing, or we feel pain. And for most of us, we will find a way to numb, distract, and avoid this pain as if our very existence relies on it.

For some that means substances. I look with compassion and love upon individuals who choose alcohol, drugs, or pornography because I know that they most likely have a lifetime of emotions that haven't been released.

The external world tells us that emotions are bad, that we should avoid them at all costs. In fact, there are thousands of pharmaceuticals to temporarily switch our body responses off if our bodies let us know that we have some stuck energy inside. We have all been conditioned to avoid pain and the signals that they provide.

I feel even more compassion for my brothers. They are told if they are strong men, they won't feel; if they do choose to feel, they are weak, they are flawed, and they aren't strong.

Bullshit. Utter bullshit.

It's time to disband the fallacy around emotions. They are simply energy in motion that allow us to feel this body and the human experience that we are in. They are our internal guidance system that helps us to stay aligned with our truth and purpose.

And the most important thing I can say in this chapter and encourage you to consider is this:

We are NOT our emotions.

Let's say that once again . . .

WE ARE NOT OUR EMOTIONS.

We *feel* our emotions and we feel this divine energy moving through us and showing us the way. When we identify with our emotions, we create anxiety and depression. And we create endless stories around them.

When we think that we are the emotions themselves, then we do everything we can to turn them off. If we are angry, it means we are out of control and there is something wrong with us. If we are sad, we need to figure out how to not feel sad and to become happy, because we are always supposed to be happy, right? And when we push those very useful (but uncomfortable) emotions away, we store them and start to cause ourselves physical symptoms, which can eventually lead to disease, or dis-ease.

As we move out of alignment and away from our truth, we will feel sensations that will help us to be consciously aware that we are moving away from our path. When we feel those higher frequencies of love, connection, peace, happiness, or expansion, we can know that we are moving toward something that will be in our highest and best benefit. However, when we have a "gut feeling" or a "knowing" inside and move away from it due to fear, laziness, or disregard, we can often feel those lower frequencies of sadness, discouragement, frustration, and even apathy. Emotions can help us achieve the best possible life when we listen to them.

Now, I know that some of you may be thinking, "But wait! What if someone breaks my heart, or I lose a loved one, or my spouse makes me angry? Those aren't emotions that guide me. They happen to me! This is real life!"

There are occasions when the Universe takes over and you are allowed a growing opportunity. But most of the time we make up stories around the situation and the emotion and that is why we have a hard time understanding their messages—we resist them instead of receiving them.

For example, when we lose a loved one, we experience grief.

It is intense grief and loss, and we have the opportunity to feel them both in their full capacity.

The only reason we feel grief is that we had the opportunity to feel love; what a beautiful reason to feel an emotion. The problem with the loss is that we make up stories like, "I cannot live without this person. I will never be the same again. I am not whole without them in my life." Yes, it may feel that way, but in reality, you will live, and you will be changed into a different version of your human self, and you are whole no matter what. The secret is to feel the emotion and let it move through you, instead of holding onto it for dear life. We may actually be fearful that when we lose that feeling, we will lose more of that person. The emotions will teach us until we are willing to learn the lesson and be done with that phase of life.

We can move past the pain and into understanding, compassion, and even gratitude.

The problem is that we fear emotions, especially the lower frequency emotions, with all of our might. Many of us will do everything to avoid them. However, when we start to discover the beauty of each emotion and embrace the fact that emotions are here to teach us, we can respect them for what they are: the internal guidance system.

This is how we start to form an alliance with emotions, rather than continuing the war we have had with them since childhood. Do you remember when your parents asked you to stop crying, or stop being angry, or stop feeling sad and "buck up"? We all learned at a young age not to feel, and that certain emotions were bad or not healthy, while others were allowable.

When an intense emotion happens, if we feel it in all the intensity, we usually only have to feel the discomfort for about 90 seconds. There are exceptions, of course, but many times we simply need to feel, and then breathe to let it go. You don't always have to analyze emotions, but if you are open, they can teach you some beautiful lessons along the way. The key is to feel.

You must feel to heal.

And then there is trauma. Every person in this world has experienced it to some degree. Anytime you experience something and rehash it over and over instead of allowing it to flow through you, you experience some sort of trauma. When the emotion of an experience has been trapped and not released, or the experience has triggered a disassociation from your body, you will have trapped emotional trauma in your body that needs to be unstuck. If it sits long enough, it will create dis-ease, and the stuck energy will show up physically.

So, where do we start in processing this stuck emotion or trauma that we didn't deal with in the moment?

There are many techniques I discuss in this book, steps I outline in the chapter on trauma, the chapter on breath, and the chapter on meditation. But I encourage you to start in this chapter with awareness. Where are you feeling the stuck energy? Do you have chronic lower back issues? Do you get sore and tight in your hips? Have you been diagnosed with things such as fibromyalgia or another auto-immune disease? Do you have depression or debilitating anxiety?

Get aware of what is going on in your body.

Start with journaling and meditating over the areas that may need to be addressed first. Journal and ponder on those areas and choose to believe that you can release that energy when you are ready to do so.

Use your heart space to make the decision on what action to take. I will outline many actions in this book, including breathwork, cold therapy, EMDR, AIT, hypnotherapy, energy work, Reiki, massage, yoga, meditation, and plant medicine.

Your answer may be outside of this list. The point is to listen to your heart and not your head and choose to take action on the option that is being presented to you.

I also have found tremendous value in reaching for a book that explains the emotional base of physical symptoms in the body. There are inspired books such as *The Healing Questions Guide*, by Wendi Jensen; Louise Hay's book, *You Can Heal your Life*, and *Feelings Buried Alive Never Die*, by Karol Truman. These books can help you tune into the root cause of where you may have buried a deep emotion. For instance, if you have trouble with your lungs, you most likely have a lot of grief stored. These books present good ideas of how you can move that trauma through affirmations and awareness, and then you can further this healing by taking action on a modality of healing that you are inspired and led to.

Now as I experience intense emotions, I have learned to sit with them and look at them with curiosity instead of disdain. I will often place one hand over my heart and one over my solar plexus (right under the ribcage) and repeat over and over, "Can I love myself through this?" (thank you Angel Lyn for teaching me this!). And yes—I can love myself through the emotion, because I am not my emotion. I am a divine individual having a human experience and I can love the emotion and the experience of that emotion regardless of the situation.

If you are like many people, it has been a very long time since you have listened to your emotions and allowed yourself to feel them. The language that they speak may be incredibly confusing to you. It is difficult to come to a place of love with your emotions if you are not aware of how they filter through your body and mind.

Many of us, especially those who have experienced sexual trauma, are completely unaware of our bodies and our emotions. Many of us separated from our bodies in an effort to protect ourselves in crisis situations. And once our lives were safe and stable, we never rejoined our bodies again.

So learning emotions will be like learning a new language. It may take time. It may take effort, but it will allow you to feel alive once again, perhaps for the first time in your life. Be patient and kind and loving as you learn this new language.

In this great age and time, there is even new technology that allows you to use your voice to help identify what emotions you are feeling at any given moment. Your voice has a frequency of the emotions you are currently experiencing. I know it sounds crazy, but this technology has been researched and patented with scientific proof that it does indeed work.

What this technology is able to do is to allow you to become very aware of how you feel when you are experiencing certain emotions, and then it guides you through techniques to flow through the emotion and then back to neutrality. It also allows you to utilize tools so you can shift into other emotions and "choose another channel."

Basically it helps you learn to have control over your emotions. You can choose to "feel it," "move it," or "change it to a new emotion." And yes, you can get so good at working with your emotions that you can choose what experience you have. Usually this kind of teamwork with emotion only comes after you have released old trauma and trapped-energy-in-motion and have learned to make peace with them. You will start learning how to flow with life and whatever the Universe brings you to learn, instead of fighting and worrying and resisting.

If this is intriguing, you can find out more information on my website and gain access to the technology through any of my programs. My mission has always been for the transformation to happen within, and not through any guru or pill or powder. It is within you, my friend. Learning how to navigate and become emotionally intelligent will change your life and allow you to make peace with intense emotions and flow with the shifts in life.

I am especially excited to help those who are between ages sixteen and twenty-five. Our teens and young adults are experiencing record numbers of suicide and depression and anxiety, and this tool can help them understand and become emotionally resilient. They can discover that emotions are not who they are, but rather their internal guidance system, and that they are in charge of their emotions.

Individuals with PTSD from military experiences and those who have been through sexual traumas will be able to get back into their bodies and learn to move these energies from their lives and into healing.

When we shift out of a place of fear and into a solid base of love toward our emotions, we become empowered and unstoppable.

You, my friend, are brave. You are courageous. You can start feeling in order to heal.

Points to Ponder:

- Become aware of your emotions. When you feel an uncomfortable feeling come up, instead of running to numb or avoid it by using technology, listen and get curious with what your emotions are saying.

- Journal and dialogue to yourself on areas of tension in your body and discover where that trapped energy is being stored. Again, listen and become aware.

- Listen to your heart space and take one small step to discover modalities that may help you let go of that trapped emotion.

- The voice technology/emotional intelligence app is explained on my website. Feel free to dive into the research and information about this useful tool that can help you become more emotionally intelligent and resilient.

Chapter 6
TRUTH ABOUT FEMININE AND MASCULINE ENERGY

I walked into the conference room. The tables were set up to accommodate 650 women from all cultures, all nationalities, all ethnicities, and all financial statuses. We were all in one room, sitting together, linking arms, and raising each other up.

This was my version of heaven: where individuals recognize and connect with what they have in common, instead of focusing on what is different; where women could show the side that comes so naturally to them . . . the "gathering side." It is what we are naturally designed to do, and that is why we women feel so incredibly amazing when we get together, when we ensure that there is no gossiping or backbiting—that only encouragement is felt and uplifting words are spoken.

This day would prove to be one of my top ten experiences to date. Each speaker walked onto stage and shared both their heart and their words, which resonated with each one of us. We danced to "This is Me," and loved and laughed together. The theme of the conference was "You Got This," and the intent was to encourage women to recognize that they indeed do more things right than wrong (the wrong they so often cling to in order to prove they aren't "good enough.")

My intent with every word I write and every presentation I give is to instill hope and healing in the hearts and minds of the people I am with.

On this day, I knew that my intention had been pure.

I believe that using your spiritual gifts is the most fulfilling thing you can do during your life here on Earth. This is how you stop choosing to make a living and start choosing to create a life.

I used my spiritual gifts and received the power of peace and joy and love that I had not experienced so fully before this conference.

I was on an incredible natural high that comes after accomplishing something really important and special. These conferences were incredibly special for me and after participating in four conferences back-to-back, it was time to go home and rest.

These conferences had taken everything I had and . . . I was tired.

No, let's rephrase that. I was exhausted beyond any exhaustion I had ever experienced.

I don't remember how I even got home. It was a three-hour drive and somehow an angel carried me on their back, because I honestly don't recall that ride home.

As I walked into my home, my bag was so incredibly heavy in my hand. I dropped it to the ground and looked up at the staircase that seemed to go on forever. In my mind, I realized that when I got to the top of the stairs, I would reach my room and finally get the rest that my body was screaming for.

Each step it took more and more effort to simply raise my foot and get to the next tread. I stopped halfway to catch my breath and asked God to help me get to my bedroom.

I had just reached the top of the landing and turned left toward my room, when suddenly my knees gave out and I collapsed into a heap on the floor. I heard a "zing" in my head and I started rocking gently back and forth and back and forth on the floor, knowing that nothing would ever be the same for me again.

This began my health journey. In all of my experiences, this one would prove to be the Mount Everest of challenges for me.

I am pretty sure I have spent hundreds of thousands of dollars in my pursuit of the answers I need to help my body to heal and to support my body in ways I have never shown up for myself before.

My body radiated with excruciating pain from head to toe. I would learn words to describe my symptoms, words such as tinnitus, vertigo, brain fog, fibromyalgia, Hashimoto's, leaky gut, SIBO, chronic UTI, and cystitis.

At the beginning of my health journey, I could only eat a handful of things—usually only cooked vegetables and some lean protein—because I became allergic to almost everything. Food, supplements, pharmaceuticals—my body would hyper react to just all of them.

I felt trapped in a body that was rebelling and I couldn't stop the train ride.

At that time, I would describe it as the train ride to hell, but later I learned that this was one of the greatest gifts that had ever entered my life. It taught me the lessons I needed in order to create differently and to love myself through this journey.

On the other side of this opportunity for healing, I recognized the energy I had used to put on those conferences.

The energy was one of proving—proving my worth to myself, to others, and most of all, to God. I wanted Him to see that I was doing everything in my power to do the right things and to show Him my love.

The biggest problem was that I didn't trust anyone else in the conference preparation process. I didn't trust the others helping me. I didn't trust that they would get their part of the process done, so I simply took over because their inaction validated my "story." I am certain that they would have completed their assignments had I simply allowed space and a trusting and loving heart for them to show up in. I didn't trust that the Universe would provide what I needed for my creation to come together in the perfect manner it was supposed to. And I didn't trust myself to see that the conference would come together without me hustling to make it happen.

So I drove myself into the ground trying to do a "good thing."

How many of us do this: drive ourselves to be completely empty because we are trying to do good things in our lives?

But we do. We try to please everyone else in an effort to be a good person, and we end up draining ourselves of everything we have to offer. And so we show up in the tired and overwhelmed and frustrated version of ourselves, instead of in the compassionate and loving version that could connect us with our loved ones, if only we would change the energy behind our actions.

So my body was the vessel of truth and light that showed me that I wasn't creating in a manner that was sustainable. It showed me that it couldn't take the stored energy inside that I was constantly feeding it: the energy of frustration, self-betrayal, and stuffing down my words because I didn't want to speak the truth.

It's better to be polite, right? It seemed better not to cause any waves of tension in my life, so I thought it was easier to not speak and to simply give what I didn't have to give anymore.

I am so incredibly grateful for my body's response. Our bodies don't lie. They can't lie. They simply show us where we are off course in our lives. And I was off course in a big way. Even though I thought I was doing such an incredible service to humanity, I was doing it in a frenzy with a hustle energy. I can't imagine being my partner or colleague in that stage of my life because I am certain I had a constant whip out to ensure everything was getting done.

Fear was behind all of my actions and I leaned in big-time to that fear.

And my body was telling me it wouldn't support this energy anymore.

What does your body tell you? Is it showing you that you may have an opportunity to show up in a creative flow using your feminine energy instead of the driving nature of the masculine?

Listen, listen. What does it tell you? What does it say?

Does it ask for you to release what no longer serves you? Is it telling you that your lifestyle is not in alignment with what your desires are? Does it tell you that you have some thinking errors?

After constant searching for four years, I discovered some things my body was telling me.

First, my adrenal glands were tanked. They were completely dried out with nothing else to give. It wasn't simply the conferences, but add to those conferences my stressful real estate business, my family, my church callings (assignments), and my constant to-do list, and I had a recipe for destruction.

As I used supplements and rest to start healing my adrenal glands, I also learned that as a holistic being, I am not just my physical body. I am also an emotional, mental, and spiritual being. So in order to heal, it was important to address all parts of me, and to find the reason I felt so compelled to prove to the world that I was of value.

So I searched for the answers. What are my adrenal glands trying to say to me?

I love inspired books that help enlighten and assist us in understanding this language of the body.

One of my favorites is Wendi Jensen's "The Healing Questions Guide."

Our brain is wired to answer questions, so when we ask our body and mind questions, they will respond with an answer.

One example Jensen uses in her book is the case of adrenal depletion. Here are the questions she suggests asking:

- What do I need to take care of myself better?
- What would it take to fill me up with joy and laughter?
- Who can help me with these burdens?
- What will it take for me to delegate some of the responsibilities I have placed on myself that can be borne to others?

Interesting, isn't it?

It's no wonder that so many women have adrenal issues. We live in a society where it isn't acceptable to receive help, but only to give and show what a badass we are.

Women were never supposed to show up this way. We are receivers in nature. Think about how human life is created. Women *receive* the sperm that the male *gives.*

Masculine energy is all about doing and achieving and giving. Males were designed to be our protectors. And while both sexes have both masculine and feminine energies, if we become lopsided in one energy that isn't a part of our original gender and makeup, we will have health issues, emotional issues, and an inability to receive the joy we are supposed to experience in this life.

When women regained some of their power in the mid-20th century, we dove right into masculine energy full force. We were proving that we could do everything that males can do.

And guess what?

We proved it.

But with that proof came a huge price to pay. Many women are tired, burned out, discouraged, frustrated, and resentful of their lives. They feel tired nonstop and can't understand why they can't feel good again.

When you look at their lifestyles, you see them going nonstop, wearing ten different hats per day, and doing, doing, and doing some more. Most women work outside of the home *and* juggle work, family, church, and personal lives. And they are teaching their future generations to "do" by signing them up for every possible sports team, music lesson, dance lesson, and academic opportunity imaginable. So many are scared that if they get this thing called "parenthood" wrong, they will realize that they really aren't good enough, which is their deepest fear.

So, fear drives this incessant hamster-wheel of life, needing to do more, have more, and become more.

And . . . it's killing us. It is burning us into the ground.

Divine feminine energy is not about doing, but being. It is about flowing and creating and having pleasure and joy. It is about compassion and love and freedom.

And driving ourselves into the ground is anything but being loving and compassionate with ourselves.

In 2012, the Mayan calendar ended and it was the beginning of a new time in history. This new time is shifting many women into remembering our divine femininity and stepping into the role of being fully alive and fully feminine. We use the masculine energy to get things done, but that isn't our primary way of functioning.

As I am writing this book, I am still working on healing tired adrenals. But I love them so much for showing me the utter madness of my former lifestyle. When I put on the conference I described above, I did so with massive "push" energy. I remember even saying that I would go door to door selling tickets if I had to. This is not flow energy; this isn't doing business intuitively and using that "knowing" that women are gifted with to create. Thus my adrenal glands were overworked, out of balance, and finally couldn't do it anymore.

Most autoimmune issues and inflammation are caused by overworked adrenal glands. And most people with autoimmune problems are women . . . interesting. Is there a correlation? Are we showing up in life trying to prove to everyone that we are valuable, rather than remembering that we always have been? Do we believe what the world has programmed us to believe—that we will only feel satisfaction when we have attained everything outside of ourselves—rather than remembering the truth of who we are and then learning to live life in trust and flow again?

As I heal my adrenals, I am learning to flow once again. I show up in business much differently. I only work with clients that honor and respect me, instead of working with everyone through a scarcity mindset. I work with intuition, instead of pushing energy and throwing-spaghetti-on-the-wall-to-see-what-sticks type of energy. My business is flourishing like never before.

I show up at home with joy again. I put on music and dance and laugh like I haven't in years. I am in "arousal" now, which is not just sexual arousal. It is being aware of the sunlight on my back and the beautiful warmth that I feel. It is snuggling with my little dog and feeling his love and the softness of his hair. It is watching my granddaughter play pretend with her stuffed animals and seeing her animation on display. It is feeling the soapy warmth of the water as I wash dishes. It is "feeling" everything, and being in that childlike awe once again.

Even in writing this book, I am choosing to create in pleasure. I look forward to each morning as I rise and start my day aligning with Source through meditation and prayer. I finish my morning ritual with smelling my choice of essential oil (I use Melissa each morning, but there are many who use Rosemary or a different oil that they feel is right for them), then intentionally imagining light going through my body, pushing out of my feet and wrapping around me and then sealing back up at my feet. I then ask for my angels and mentors from the other side to be with me, and then I am ready to create.

My old self would have gotten very impatient with this process and thought it was a time waster. I would have written my book as fast as I could, staying up until the wee hours of the morning in order to get it done.

The new me understands the power of aligning and connecting with Source Energy before I create anything. The morning ritual creates a space in which I can create with joy and pleasure and it doesn't feel like work; it feels like love. In this energy, I am leaning into love instead of fear. It doesn't matter how long it takes to write this book—it will be done when it is supposed to be done. I can use my masculine energy to ensure that this morning time is non-negotiable and to take the time each morning to visit with my book, but the creation is in feminine energy.

I also show up for myself in love by making sure I don't "do it all." I can ask for help and I can receive it gladly, realizing that this effort isn't proving my worth, but loving what is already whole.

I have learned to hire things out that are added to my "to-do" list mentality. I hire a cleaner every two weeks; I get delivery service for groceries; I take naps when I am tired. I am not lazy, but rather, I love my body and my adrenals more than I "love" getting things done on my own. I am not proving to anyone anymore that I am worthwhile because I can do it all. I am valuable because of who I am.

I have remembered and awakened from a deep slumber.

I am done "doing" my way to gaining the approval of the world or of a God who loves me anyway.

Are you ready to stop the insanity and to slow down enough to take care of the only you there is?

Are you ready to create out of pleasure and allow yourself to show up in love for others instead of in the tired and frustrated version of yourself?

Can you trust that you can actually create more while doing less? That in working with the divine feminine energy, it is possible to come up with creative answers that you would have overlooked if you had kept busy in the hustle and frenzy of life?

Life is to be experienced in pleasure. Life is meant to be felt and noticed and love is meant to return to your heart.

This life is always showing up for you. You can look at what is coming to you with eyes of fear or with eyes of love. The choice is yours. If you choose to see with love, you will discover the lessons unfolding and a new, higher version of yourself emerging from the layers of the lies of yesterday.

Points to Ponder:

- If you are currently living life in constant motion, decide on one thing you can cut out of your life right now. Do your children really need to be involved in five extracurricular activities, or could you cut one of those out? Could you carve a small portion of money out of your budget to cover house cleaning once or twice per month?

- Self-care is a modern buzzword, and too many people find a way to make it a part of their to-do list along with everything else in their lives. The key to self-care is finding something that makes your heart soar when you think about it. It could be as easy as sitting in a bubble bath without any distractions. It could be a slow walk around the block and noticing the beauty in nature. It doesn't have to be a spa day or doing something that costs money. It could even be writing in your journal. Think of something that makes you feel good. It is all about bringing pleasure back into your life. When you learn how to bring pleasure into one area, you will start to notice how that feels and find other ways to bring more into your life.

- Choose to create an ethereal moment in the mundane tasks that you do each day. If you are washing your hands, feel the soap on your hands and the warmth of the water as you rinse your hands under the faucet—be present and feel the beauty in that moment.

- Find a routine or a practice that works well for you as a way to start each day. Instead of darting out of bed and starting the craziness off from the moment you wake up, learn to align with Source Energy as your first priority. This will allow you to create your life with help from the divine. It is much easier to navigate in that space.

Chapter 7
TRUTH ABOUT BREATH

I was on the floor in my bedroom. I had been asked to get a blanket and to be as comfortable as possible. It was dark and I was surrounded by my most familiar items—the ones that bring me comfort and familiarity.

As part of an online retreat that I was speaking at, I had been invited to experience breath work. I thought I knew what that meant; I mean, I had practiced yoga for almost thirty years and loved the way ujjayi breathing could help me remain present and focused as the cool air passed through my constricted throat on an inhale and then back out on an exhale, creating a sort of meditative experience.

But here I was, on the floor, starting to feel a buzz glide over my body around the seven-minute mark of breathing twice in my mouth, the first one from using my belly and the second in my diaphragm, and then exhaling one breath out. The energy was so intense in my hands that they started to form claws, cramping and twisting into a weird shape. My knees started to shake and shiver as if I were in a subzero climate.

What the hell was happening to me?

And that is when I felt the ball of energy rise to my throat. It wasn't going to be trapped anymore. It came out in wave after wave of intense tears and grief that I hadn't felt in years.

And I cried, I wailed, and I felt so many emotions that had been tucked away in the sealed storage of my heart. I had stored those emotions there deliberately because I was so intensely afraid of feeling.

Because if I started feeling . . . would it ever stop? And it was too much—there was too much—and I didn't trust that I could do it.

Most of us have been told not to feel. If we started to cry as a child, we were told to stop or someone would give us a good reason to cry. If we were angry, we were sent to the corner until we stopped feeling. If we were sad, we were told to look on the bright side.

But here I was feeling . . . feeling the things that my body was finally releasing that I thought was too much for me to handle. It was intense, and freeing, and magnificent.

It was safe to feel.

I needed to feel in order to heal.

The facilitator led us through a meditation after breathing. She helped us to get back into our bodies and then gently guided us back to a place of neutrality.

At that moment, I discovered the power of breath.

Our breath is one of the only autonomic functions that we have control over.

What if I told you that breathing exercises were so powerful that they can change the PH of your blood and make it more alkaline or acidic?

What if I told you that breathwork is so powerful that it can lower your heart rate and cortisol levels and help you sleep?

What if this same exercise, in a more rigorous pattern, could have LSD-type effects and even produce out-of-body type experiences?

And all of this is done without anything but the breath.

God is so good. Everything we need for our healing and our well-being was provided from the day we took our first breath.

Jay Shetty described the lesson he learned about the importance of breath during his first day at a monastery. He observed a group of ten-year-olds and saw that the teacher was teaching this group of kids their first lesson: understanding breath.

Shetty explained that the only thing that never changes from the time we are born until the time we step into the next life is our breath.

When we are angry, what changes internally? Our breath. When we are scared or anxious, what changes? Our breath. When we are happy, what changes? Our breath.

Understanding our breath can help us to get back to a place of neutrality and peace, just by changing our breath patterns. This single realization can change the way we react to the stressors of life each day. It can help move more uncomfortable emotions from the feeling stage to the healing stage quickly and with less intensity.

It's incredible to know that if we learn how to breathe, we have the ability to navigate through life in a more effortless way.

Still not convinced?

Think about women in childbirth. What is the single thing that they are all taught in order to relax more and let the body have more effective contractions, thus lessening the pain associated with childbirth?

And if breath can help us in the most intense situations, could it not be intentional in day-to-day life?

Think about our current lives. We are a digitally-obsessed and escape-based society at this time in human history. We should be ecstatic that we have access to just about any information that we could possibly want or learn, but as a society, we are deeply unhappy.

We have record numbers of depression and anxiety cases and it is reported that these two diagnoses combined are the number one disability in the world. It doesn't surprise anyone that 25% of people are on an antidepressant of some sort and that sleep deprivation is at an epidemic level right now.

Our busy lives are not sustainable. Given the opportunity to talk with one of the individuals who seems to have it all put together and is running a company, you may be surprised to learn that these "put-together" people can't sleep, they have panic attacks, and they are chronically depressed.

We cannot sustain this lifestyle anymore. It isn't possible and we owe it to our children to help them learn differently, to learn better. We do not want to pass on this insane lifestyle to our future generations. But how do they learn unless they see our example on how to do things differently?

Breath, my friends.

Breath can absolutely change your life and create a huge shift for you in reacting differently to various stimuli and returning you back to your natural state, which is peaceful and non-reactionary to what is happening around you.

In this day and age where it appears that everything is falling apart, we can keep our nervous systems in check and learn to breathe with different emotions and in the challenges that come our way, and we can feel empowered instead of out of control.

What are the basics?

Well for starters, you will need to learn how to breathe from your belly instead of from your chest.

Most Americans are chest breathers. This type of breath is helpful when you are in fight and flight and need to be on high alert. It is, however, not the way that we are supposed to breathe when we are in our parasympathetic nervous system, which is where we should be most of the time. When we feel peace and harmony, we are in this part of our nervous system.

The first and most important way to breathe is a three-part breath. Breathe into your belly first and watch it go up to your rib cage and then finally reach your chest. Breathe out with that same pattern on the exhale. Watch your breath go out of your chest and down your ribcage and then out your belly.

This breath pattern will help you begin the process of returning to your body and melding it with your mind and spirit. This is the beginning of feeling peace and bliss and returning to wholeness. Isn't it amazing and yet so simple?

You can use a four-count breath pattern and teach yourself how to breathe properly again. Do this anytime you think about it during the day. We generally breathe in a two-count breathing pattern, and so by simply increasing it to a four-count inhalation and a four-count exhalation, you will begin to see a shift in your nervous system.

For sleep or when you choose to really relax, you can do a more intentional pattern of breathing that will help you rest and recover. It is called the 4-7-8 breathing pattern. Military professionals—like snipers or Navy SEALs going into a chaotic situation— use this technique as they go into situations in which they need focus. The military only uses methods that work, so if it works under extreme stress, most likely it can help you as well. This method is simply breathing in for a count of four, holding for a count of seven, and breathing out for a count of eight. Simple.

Another way to use breath for healing is to utilize a method of controlled stress to help you teach your body that, even though it is used to telling you that it's under threat, since you can now regulate and control this action, you also know how to return it to homeostasis. The more you teach your brain that your spirit is in control and not the latter, the less anxiety and stress you will feel.

With the more extreme breathing techniques, you can actually help your body to release trauma. It makes sense that I cried so many tears during my first intense breathwork session. I came to understand that grief is stored in the lungs; when we don't feel grief and instead stuff it down, it will end up being stored in the lungs. And so when we breathe, or rather when we *intentionally* breathe in certain patterns, our breath helps us release that old stored emotion that we have buried deep within.

Stanford did a research study about breathwork with veterans diagnosed with PTSD. The researchers worked with the veterans for three months and at the end of the study, they showed that the PTSD had been released and didn't show back up even a year later. This is an especially profound result considering that every day, over twenty veterans end their own lives.

Breathwork has the capacity to change our society.

I love watching things unfold that will help us when we are ready. I am not surprised at how many options there are for us to learn controlled breathing patterns and have them at our fingertips.

The basic concept of breathwork is that you will learn a breath pattern that you will control for thirty seconds to several minutes. Many breathwork teachers will have you exhale and then hold your breath for up to ninety seconds. Those of you who struggle with holding your breath on the exhale for longer than thirty seconds will most likely have some adrenal function compromised. The good news is that you will find many sections in this book that will help you to reclaim those beautiful adrenals and learn to pivot some aspects in your life so that you won't have that issue again. You will find that you start to flow more and hustle less.

For years, I struggled with panic attacks. Interestingly, I had never had a panic attack until *after* I was prescribed an antidepressant many years ago (I have been off that medication for a decade now).

It is also not surprising that the panic attacks started happening right after the death of my father. The panic attacks were my body's way of showing me that my deep grief was trapped and ready to be released. Until I learned the power of breath, I would wake up in the middle of the night experiencing a panic attack and would take a Xanax to calm me down.

Now if I ever wake up in the middle of the night with a panic attack (which I haven't actually experienced for years), I simply exhale first, as this is the way to tell your body you are safe. Think about when we see a beautiful rainbow or see a baby for the first time . . . we sigh and breathe out. If we are about to be hit by a bus, we inhale sharply and tense our body. So exhale first. Then you can focus on the four-square method I mentioned above, in which you inhale for a count of four, hold for a count of four, then exhale for a count of four, and hold for a count of four. I try to get myself up to a count of ten at each point of the "square." The longer the breath, the more the mind and nervous system believes you are safe—you couldn't possibly be running—and you return to homeostasis.

Unbelievable, but true.

Deep diaphragmatic breaths will bring you back to your body in love and the fear will leave. Fear cannot exist in the presence of love. Breathwork is one of the greatest ways to rediscover and remember who you really are.

The benefits are far more expansive than helping with *just* anxiety, though. Breath acts as an antidepressant, lowers blood pressure, helps you sleep better, improves your immune response, helps with autoimmune problems and digestive issues, and alleviates chronic stress.

Sounds like the cure for the modern world, doesn't it?

It is magical, especially the first time you try it.

When I hold my breath and squeeze it from the base of my spine up to my head, a magical rush of energy guides me into one of the deepest forms of meditation that I have ever experienced. It is a beautiful glow that I feel all over my body, almost as if I have had a spiritual hug and kiss and I feel refreshed, alive, and full of energy once again.

I love to pair breath with cold therapy. Wim Hof was the first person to really shed light on the power of the cold, though he never really wanted to be the "poster child" of this movement. However, his unique style and personality drew attention to the "crazy iceman." And there is scientific research that what he does actually works.

Every day, Wim would walk across the street and walk into the freezing cold pond. He found it to be therapeutic for both his physical body and his mental state. He paired this practice with his breath and found that the therapeutic benefits filtered into every aspect of his life.

One day, as a local TV crew was filming him getting into the cold water, someone fell through the ice. Wim promptly drew in his breath, ducked under the ice, and held his breath for four minutes as he swam to save the person. He then inhaled another breath, ducked back under the ice, and held his breath for another four minutes as he swam back to where he had started. This was all caught on camera, and all of sudden, Wim was famous.

He also participated in a study where a hundred individuals were injected with E. Coli to see how the immune system responded. He was the only one out of over one hundred test subjects who did not get sick. Puzzled, the scientists asked what he did differently.

His response? Breath and mindset.

The next step was allowing him to teach others the same method and then allowing them to participate in the same research on E. Coli and the immune system. The results? Every person who used breath and mindset was able to resist bacterial infection.

Breath . . . it can impact our immune system.

Can you imagine what else they will discover it has the power to influence?

It is the single most powerful force we have available to help us feel good in this world.

Learn to control your breath, and learn to be intentional in the life you choose to live.

A list of clinically studied benefits are:

- lower blood pressure
- lower cortisol level (this is what increases your stress response)
- better sleep
- lower anxiety
- lower depression rate
- healthier immune response
- enhanced memory
- promoting of weight loss
- increased bone density

Now these are the benefits that are backed up by research and data. However, I can tell you that each time I experience breathwork, I feel amazing benefits. The physical benefits are tangible, but the sense of well-being, peace, and coming back to myself are what I really get excited about.

The other huge benefit that I want to mention, due to the healing effects breath has in our lives, is the power to bring up stored emotion and to release it through the breath.

Throughout this book, I will continually discuss releasing emotions and trauma, and you are welcome for that. If you learn nothing more from this book than ways to release stored trauma and emotions, your life will change. Stored trauma and emotion form a wall that blocks you from experiencing your best life.

I am intentionally starting with the chapter on breathwork prior to the chapter on meditation. It is incredibly difficult for a person who is in fight and flight to sit down and calm their mind. However, when that same individual starts with learning how to breathe and practice intentional breathwork, they can then sit easily in meditation and start learning the benefits of that practice and connection to self.

With all of this hype, are you ready to try this out for yourself?

Here are some resources to help you start your journey. I do recommend working with someone who has training and understanding before choosing the breathwork you will practice. There are some risks involved with individuals prone to seizures or who take heavy medications, so please be aware of those risks prior to engaging in a breathwork practice.

Points to Ponder:

- Basic breathing techniques can be powerful. Start with a four-square breathing pattern, and feel the benefits immediately. Breathe in for a count of four, hold for a count of four, breathe out for a count of four, and hold for a count of four. Throughout the day consciously practice breathing in and out at a four-count pace.

- Use the 4-7-8 technique to help you relax and sleep at night.

- Utilize intentional breathwork. I suggest you find a facilitator for your first experiences because they will hold a safe space and guide you through the process. If any trauma or intense emotions are brought up, they can help you feel safe to do work through those traumas or emotions.

- Start slow and work up. Don't begin your practice with advanced techniques, holding your breath longer than ninety seconds to two minutes. Help your system work up to that level and begin with gentler practice. Do not practice holds if you have a history of seizures. Always consult with your medical professional before starting any new practice.

Chapter 8
TRUTH ABOUT MEDITATION

I walked down the stairs from the stage. I had just spoken about the power of a morning routine, a detailed version of a step-by-step approach to have a fantastic day.

What a crock of crap.

It was the worst presentation I had ever given.

I'm not going to sugar coat it. It sucked.

In addition to the AV tech completely disappearing and not having access to anything to help me with my guided meditation, I was off. I was so off that the emcee actually tried saving the presentation by interjecting some additional support for my epically-failing guided meditation.

But there was more to it than that.

I knew in my heart that there wasn't one certain way to do anything. My recipe of life by that time was already dismantling. I realized quickly that the reason that so many individuals who went to conference after conference seeking ways to finally "get life right" never received the exact method that would work for them, was that what they learned wasn't "their" recipe. It wasn't their way to align with Source. It wasn't their way to create. They loved the feeling of getting all pumped up and leaving on cloud nine, but when they got back to real life, they would realize that the long list of to-dos would be neither sustainable nor enjoyable.

I had just delivered yet another to-do list to the never-ending hustle they were already living.

And I knew in my whole being that there was another way.

The only time my life seemed to go in the right direction was when I listened to my heart.

There was no system. There was no ideal way. There was just my way, with God by my side.

What the people needed was to hear their own voice again, not the voice of another person. That is why it didn't work, why it could only be sustainable for a short amount of time.

Plus, my eyelashes were literally falling off of my face. And I had worn black, and the backdrop was black, so it appeared as if I was a floating head on stage.

Yep, it was a train wreck.

I immediately started toward the bathroom and realized that wearing a jumpsuit to an all-day conference was also not a smart idea.

As I was washing my hands, I looked over and caught the eye of a beautiful redhead. She noticed my eyelash hanging by a thread and we both busted out laughing.

She complimented my presentation and also had pity for the AV that was nonexistent, and then she said, "You know, there is something you could add to your morning routine that would change your life."

Being the curious person that I am, I asked what that might be.

"Kundalini Yoga could change your life," she said.

Three times. I had heard "Kundalini Yoga" three times in the previous month. I knew how messages were sent to me; sometimes it took three times for me to really remember and pay attention. When I hear something multiple times consecutively, it is almost always something for me to learn, something important for me to take notice of. So I looked up toward heaven and winked. "Yes, I believe it would change my life to learn Kundalini Yoga. Would you teach it to me?" I asked her.

That night, my new friend Hollie taught another woman and me some basic Kundalini mantras—tuning in and learning a new language of chanting. I felt a little awkward and out of my element as I chanted and sang, but I felt something switch on in me. When I used the vibration of my voice, I felt different. I felt somehow more alive, like I was channeling wisdom and light right through my voice and fingertips.

Kundalini Yoga was brought to America by an enlightened teacher named Yogi Bhajan. Up until then, this technology was only known and passed down from royal lineage in the Middle East. Yogi Bhajan arrived in America during the 1960s at a time when many young people were using drugs to have "spiritual experiences." Yogi Bhajan explained that they could have the same experiences they were having with substances by using only the mind, the body, and the breath. He called it the 3HO (healthy, happy, holy) way of life.

When asked why he chose to bring this technology to the western world he stated, "You live in a desert and I have some water."

Water.

The only substance outside of ourselves that we can't live without.

Interesting that this technology could bring spiritual water to the desert.

We live in one of the greatest financially abundant civilizations in the world, but because we are spiritually starving and dehydrated, we are always searching for answers outside of ourselves, even though we have so many techniques to discover it within ourselves.

We also live in a world where we are constantly bombarded with stimuli. Our nervous systems were not designed to handle that much data, and so the majority of us feel tired and foggy. We often feel like we are "short-circuiting," so to speak.

Yogi Bhajan knew that in the age of Aquarius (which is the time we live in), we indeed would need something to calm our nervous systems.

Kundalini Yoga quenched my spiritual thirst and calmed my frazzled nervous system in a way that nothing else had up to that point.

It taught me to quiet the mind so the soul can speak.

I remember trying this so-called "meditation" thing for years and leaving the pillow feeling more frustrated than I had been when I began. The thoughts were on a never-ending loop of madness, harassing me until I listened.

They never stopped harassing.

I tried guided meditations and those seemed to work better. I definitely improved my skills, and I personally even taught simple and basic guided meditations to get individuals into gratitude, which is an active form of love. When we can shift into gratitude, we change our vibration.

But I still fell short on this meditation gig.

And now this "weird chanting yoga," as my husband lovingly referred to it . . . was working.

It quieted my mind like nothing else had ever done.

For instance, one of the many Kundalini kriyas—the Kirtan Kriya—uses sound, touch, and vibration to gently lull the consciousness into a clear and blissful state of mind. Each time you touch the tip of your finger with the thumb you chant a different sound.

Sa, Ta, Na, Ma ... Sa, Ta, Na, Ma ... Sa, Ta, Na, Ma.

Birth, life/growth, death/change, rebirth.

The stages of life. The stages of growth. The stages in which we shed old beliefs and trauma.

At first the sound is singing in a regular tone of voice, next in a whisper, then silently, back to a whisper, and finally singing at a normal volume once again. These can be done in two-minute cycles when you are first starting out, and increased in length up to fifteen minutes per cycle.

Your sound is unique. There is no other sound like yours in the Universe. It is your universal thumbprint. According to Felice Austin (author of *Awake as in Ancient Days: The Christ-Centered Kundalini Yoga Experience*), when you use your voice as an instrument, the following positive changes occur:

- Your heart rate decreases.
- Your blood pressure decreases.
- Your stress/fear hormone decreases.
- Your body releases more endorphins.

Isn't it amazing and miraculous that we have everything inside of us that we need in order to heal? One of the tools of healing is our very own voice, and you have already learned about breath and the power of healing through the breath.

Combining our voices with the voices of others allows us to have even more power. We can become one voice and allow ourselves to have the power of raising all of our vibrations together. A live Kundalini class is like nothing I have ever experienced before.

At the end of every Kundalini class, you will always end with Satnam.

Satnam means "I am truth; truth is my identity."

It is interesting that the very name of this book would correlate with the most basic Kundalini mantra.

Learning this technology has the power of bringing you back to your truth: the only thing that exists. The only conference you will ever be required to attend, the only recipe you will ever need to save you, has always been your truth.

And this is the core of this book: that the truth is inside of you. I pray that as you read the words in the chapters beyond this one, that it will be obvious where I am taking you.

I am simply taking you home to where you always have yearned to be.

Meditation has the power to do this.

Kundalini was where I started to go within. After I had been struggling with chronic pain for years, I had experiences while practicing Kundalini Yoga where I literally felt angels touch my back. That was my only solace from a body and mind that was going through the breakdown process before rebuilding and breaking through to the other side.

Meditation allows us to drift back from the mind and body and merge back into our souls.

There are so many modalities of meditation, so it is simply your choice what calls to you most. Choose whatever can allow you to drift back into your soul once again and remind you of the truth that has always been there.

You may find other meditations incredibly healing. Michael Singer, author of *The Untethered Soul: Journey Beyond Yourself,* started his journey back to himself as he practiced Zen meditation. This type of meditation uses deep belly humming on the exhale. Other meditation practices will simply have you focus on the exhale, but the concentration on the breath will help you just like the fingers and chanting helped me in Kundalini Yoga.

Another great teacher of meditation and self-realization is Paramahansa Yogananda. His method includes the use of energizing activation techniques to calm the body and mind prior to sitting in meditation. His program is outlined very deliberately into lessons on his website, so if you need a bit of hand holding, that could be a great tool and resource for you. It's rumored that his book, *Autobiography of a Yogi*, was the only book that Steve Jobs carried with him everywhere he went. I respect the creative genius of Steve Jobs, and so I often will follow the fruits and look for the roots so that I can follow a similar path.

With that being said, I encourage you to never follow anything before going within and ensuring that this is the path that your heart wants to take. Why waste time and effort on something that isn't resonating at the highest frequency within you? There are so many technologies and ways to get into that deep meditative state. The secret is to find something you love and stick with it until you see the spiritual, mental, emotional, and physical benefits.

My first introduction to meditation was through yoga.

I grew up in the era when Jane Fonda came out with the very first workout video. I was eleven and my brother used to call me "little fatty," and so I started to work out every single day with that workout video. After a year or so, I noticed another video that came out by Raquel Welch. Little did I know that when she was talking about postures and poses, I was practicing yoga. All I knew was that it was the most challenging workout I had ever done. But doing it consistently started to shift me internally, even at that young age. I felt fantastic after doing those workouts. Later in my life, I would learn the benefits of linking breath with movement and forming that body, mind, and spirit connection.

If meditation is painful and you avoid it like the plague, start with practicing the principles from the chapter on breath and allow your nervous system to calm. Then consider Kundalini, which will use the power of your voice and breath to help you get into a meditative state on your own. If that isn't your jam, then consider other forms of yoga. I love Yin yoga or restorative yoga, and both of these will help you to learn how to quiet that voice inside.

Hiking is a form of active meditation and is one of my favorite ways to connect with the earth and my heart space. Many of my "God downloads" happen while I am hiking.

The Time2Heal video depicts one of the most private parts of my life, and the vision of that video unfolded on one of these sacred hikes. I saw it unfold in detail as I looked up and swore at God, saying, "Are you effing kidding me?"

Maybe you have seen it? Maybe that very video brought you right here to this book so that it could unfold something valuable to you. Thank goodness for God dares and action toward something that doesn't make sense.

Meditation of any sort is incredible. Most individuals starting a practice for the first time find it much more enjoyable to be doing something physical until they can start learning the spirit-mind-body connection without moving.

And that is when things get really interesting.

All of the peace and belonging and acceptance is waiting for you on the other side, or perhaps I should say, on the inside. It never left you, not even for a second.

It's like being inside for years and finally venturing out to feel the sun again. The sun never left—you simply closed the door to receiving its rays. Nature doesn't go away if you don't choose to bask in her beauty, and when you finally return, she is there waiting with open arms for you to discover her greatness again.

Every person I have ever met who seemed to be at peace with themselves and had gotten to a state of self-realization, has practiced a consistent meditative experience.

Every.Single.One.

It is one of the most important things that I believe I can offer you in this book.

I mean, how do you discover the truth inside if you never look? If you keep yourself too busy making a living or running children around to endless activities, when will you have time for you? When will it ever be your time?

My suggestion is to start with five minutes of a practice every single day. Do one of the activities listed below, and start to remember the truth as it has always been. This practice will eventually be so delicious that you won't want to skip it. It will be better than any series on Netflix, better than any rush you get from getting a new client, better than the times your child has scored a soccer goal.

Let's start the path right now. Your soul has called you to this book for a reason. It is time to remember and drift back to that knowing inside.

Where to start:

Choose from the following activities and be consistent for the next twenty-one days. Have it be as non-negotiable as brushing your teeth. Do the activity for five minutes or longer. I suggest doing this first thing in the morning, before things get rushed. Wake up a few minutes before you normally would and focus on being with you, showing up for you, and loving you.

Point to Ponder:

- Walk or hike and notice everything around you. Be in the present noticing colors, wind, smells, birds, temperature. When thoughts come up, simply notice them and allow them to fall away. Allow yourself to become "sensual" and notice every sense as you bring in the majesty of creation.

- Practice yoga. There are very good beginner videos on YouTube. A basic sun salutation moves the body and integrates it with breath, allowing you to feel that spirit-mind-body connection

- Try Kundalini Yoga. I have a basic video on my website that is about learning the Kirtan Kriya, along with "tuning in" and properly closing. Along with this, I have an interview with my teacher, Felice Austin, who shares more insight on the power of this technology—these are available both on my podcast and YouTube channels.

- Try Kriya Yoga. This type of yoga was taught originally from Paramahansa Yogananda. He has a detailed program with step-by-step instructions at www.yogananda.org. One of my mentors and teachers, Michael Singer, also practices this type of meditation. I highly recommend his books, *The Untethered Soul* and *The Surrender Experiment: My Journey into Life's Perfection*.

Chapter 9
TRUTH ABOUT PRAYER

I had just walked out of the Planned Parenthood clinic with my seventeen-year-old daughter. I thought I was going to throw up.

It was required that before an abortion, you had to take a class and since my daughter was a minor, I was required to take the class as well.

This was my daughter's decision, but every cell in my body was buzzing with resistance.

She had just discovered that she was pregnant and had been taking the drug Accutane when she conceived. Even though she was using two preventative measures, she was somehow still pregnant.

When we went to see the doctor, the first thing out of his mouth was, "You need to abort this baby. It isn't fair to the child, as it will be impacted so negatively that the quality of life will be horrific."

I didn't want to see a baby suffer, and neither did my daughter. But something seemed to be "off."

So I got down on my knees and asked. I asked God to provide the answers and the way to understand the next steps. I asked that angels surround my grieving daughter and provide strength to both of us.

The next day, my thought was to call our family practitioner to see if he could perform the abortion. That thought gave me some solace and so I dialed the phone.

Dr. Smith called me back and I explained the situation. I explained that we had talked to two doctors who had both told us the same thing: that it wasn't safe, that it wasn't in the best interest of my daughter nor the child. We even got the stamp of approval from our ecclesiastical leader that we could go ahead as planned if the doctors were suggesting it.

"Wendy, would you consider doing one thing before asking your daughter to make a decision?"

"Of course," I said.

"Let's have her meet a perinatologist that can perform an ultrasound and they will be able to help you with the knowledge she will need to move forward with a decision. And Wendy, this decision will impact your daughter's life forever. Please be mindful of the answer."

Oh yes, I would be mindful of the answer. But I also believed that my daughter would ultimately be the one to decide. In my heart was peace as I knew that we would both be led to the right decision.

A few days later my daughter, her boyfriend, my husband, and I all gathered together in a little examination room with the ultrasound machine and the doctor.

After slathering the ointment on Kelsey's belly, the doctor moved the wand around until a heartbeat could be seen beating rapidly.

A heartbeat . . .

The doctor pointed out the torso, the limbs and then . . . the kick.

The baby kicked.

I looked at my daughter, my husband, my future son-in-law, and I knew.

My husband said, "Kelsey, I don't believe we need to make a choice. The choice has already been made."

That began one of the most glorious rides of my lifetime.

As my daughter cried into my arms she said, "Mom, who is going to want a deformed baby?"

I stroked her head gently and said, "Sweetheart, I meet five beautiful couples a week that would love to raise a baby, even a special baby."

I was working as an area representative for the Utah Foster Care Foundation at the time, and my job was to ensure that the communities I served understood the need for more foster families. Since I had been a foster parent for eight years and I'd had thirteen children in my home during that time frame, I knew the highs and lows of the commitment. One of my main jobs was to meet with families in their homes to help them understand the focus on reunification and working with birth parents and the state.

Most of them desperately wanted to raise a child. They knew in their hearts that they were meant to be parents and they were open to receiving children in whatever manner they were able to come.

So I sat my beautiful daughter down at the computer. At the time, my faith of origin had an adoption agency and I had Kelsey navigate this website, looking for families that would consider special needs children. She narrowed it down to two of them, and we again went into prayer in order to find the right one.

A week later I was called to meet a family in their home, not far from my office.

As the door opened I saw a tall, slender woman with long blonde hair, wearing a beret.

She seemed so familiar. Why was that?

I brushed off the thought and sat down with the husband and wife. They seemed so cute together and laughed and bantered back and forth. There was an amazing energy in their home, and I started to relax.

I asked what they did for work. Brady started to explain that they owned a snowboard and wakeboard manufacturing company. Deborah mentioned that she had gone to her religious temple and even though they were registered at an adoption agency, she felt she needed to call the foster care people immediately.

And that is when it all started to come together.

What came together? My daughter had a family saved in her profile that owned a snowboard and wakeboard manufacturing company. I saw the banter back and forth and saw the photo on the profile pop into my head—the man with the Tom Selleck mustache on his face and the woman laughing.

It was them. I got the opportunity to interview the couple my daughter had saved in her profile and ask them any question that I wanted and they had no idea that my daughter was considering their family for adoption!

My heart started to pound so loudly that I could hear it. I kept telling myself . . . don't say anything! This isn't your decision!

But I knew. I knew in my heart that my future grandchild would be living in this home, and that these people would become a huge part of my life. I knew that love would extend beyond the current borders of my birth family, and that nothing would ever be the same again.

Right after the meeting, I was meeting Kelsey and Cameron at the base of the canyon so I could take Kelsey home. I explained the serendipitous meeting with the Fox family and Kelsey said, "Mom, if that isn't an answer to a prayer, I don't know what is."

Six months later, we encircled Kelsey's bed as she gave birth and we celebrated this life all together.

Olivia. Perfectly perfect, right from God's hands to ours. From Kelsey's unselfish arms to the Fox family's capable and loving arms.

Love in full action. Words cannot describe the miracle.

And she is a beautiful part of our lives. The last time I saw her, she ran up to me as fast as she could and embraced me in an "Olivia hug" and said, "Grandma Bunnell! Grandma Bunnell! Best grandma ever! I love you!"

Prayers answered, miracles unfolding.

The power of prayer.

The answers are always there. We simply need to ask and choose to receive the answers.

Expect the answers, and learn how God speaks to you. Learn the language of your heart.

We have angels and helpers that we can ask at any given time to help us navigate this life. We are never alone at any time.

The only requirement they have to be able to help us is that we must ask. It is a universal law and one that they are unable to cross until you reach out with a desire to be helped.

And nothing is too much to ask for. In fact, they delight in knowing that they can help you.

I was on my fiftieth-birthday trip with a group of friends when I discovered that the mortgage I had applied for wasn't going smoothly. This was stressful information because we would be homeless in less than thirty days if it didn't go through. I had an entire checklist that needed to be addressed, and it appeared that there was no way that I would be able to get everything done in the time limit I had.

Plus, I was in Mexico and wasn't interested in working.

I considered all of my options when a thought popped into my head.

"Ask for help. You cannot do this alone," the voice said.

That was when I started to pray and ask for angels to help me address each and every one of the items on the list. I was specific in assignments and duties for each one of them, and also asked for it to be done with ease and flow and for the ability to get back to the celebration with my friends. I asked for the few phone calls that were necessary to complete the list to be linked to the right person who would know exactly what I needed and be able to get it to me effortlessly.

And then I paused . . . and received my portion of the assignments. I picked up my phone, was connected with the exact person who moved through the steps easily, and assured me that I would receive the papers within the next twelve hours.

Within the day, I had the list completed. My lender was astounded at how the entire list was done in such a short amount of time.

And I got back to enjoying my trip with my friends.

I look at that experience and remember how differently I choose to experience life at this point.

Years previously, this would have ruined my trip. I would have stewed and stressed and stayed in the hotel room the whole time trying to "fix" the problem, and trying to do it all myself.

Now I know we have access to the other side with an infinite amount of help and assistance at our disposal.

This book that I am writing is not done by me. I take action in doing the work, but the words simply flow through me when I am aligned and prepared to receive the information.

I was shown a beautiful practice by my mentor and coach Keira Poulsen, which helps me get into a state of channeling rather than writing. All things are created spiritually first, and then they come into physical reality. These words are filtered through my experiences and the events that have happened in my life, but the truth never changes and the laws that apply to my situations are also laws that can help navigate yours as well.

We are never alone. Period.

I was taught at an early age that there was a proper order of prayer that must be adhered to in order to receive an answer.

I don't believe that is true. I believe that intention and opening your heart space to receive is all that is necessary.

I used to wait until I could kneel down before engaging in prayer, but I now realize I can pray anywhere, at any time, and I often do (when I am not talking to another person). I speak internally to God more than I do verbally to any human.

Can you imagine how much easier life would be if you had a continuous flow of assistance?

It is true—you do have access, and it is simply up to you to ask for it.

There are a few keys that will help you to receive and that help with more flow.

First, expect an answer. It is a law that cannot be broken. If you ask for help or an answer, you will receive it. You may not receive it in the manner you have contrived in your mind, but you will receive, nonetheless. Be open to that receiving and you will watch miracles unfold right before your eyes.

Second, be open to where the answer and support show up. Some of the time it will be almost instantaneous, but many times you will get it when you are ready to receive, or in a surprising way.

Finally, ask for help in all of your daily tasks. Are you looking to hire someone to help you with your children? Ask to be guided to the perfect person who will love your children, treat them with respect, and be dependable. Want a new career? Ask for help in guiding you to the next new opportunity that will pair well with your skillset and spiritual gifts.

Last year, I had my granddaughters come over to the house and they drew pictures and decorated envelopes to give to random strangers that we were led to. We inserted a $100 bill into each envelope and set out to a grocery store to find individuals who might need to feel more supported in life.

We started off in prayer and then I asked the girls to tune in to their hearts as to who could benefit. I encouraged them to not simply hand them out willy-nilly, but to truly tune in to the answer that they would receive inside.

The first person they spotted was sitting by the pharmacy and seemed to be in physical and emotional pain. The girls looked up at me and said, "Grandma, I think she could use some joy today!" They handed her an envelope and then we proceeded to hand out a few more.

There was one more envelope, but we all felt like it was supposed to leave the store. I thought it was strange, but I followed the promptings and left the store. I put the girls in the car and proceeded to take the grocery cart we'd used and place it back in the cart return.

That was when I saw her. I felt like I was almost pushed in her direction. I called out to her and asked if I could give her a small present that my grandchildren had made. We had one left and I felt impressed to give it to her. I also instructed her to open it right away.

I got into the car and was waiting for my daughter to come out of the store when I heard a tapping on the window. There at the window was the girl, with tears streaming down her face. I got out of the car and she asked if she could give me a hug.

I said, "Of course," and she embraced me for what seemed like a full minute or two. When she was done, she proceeded to tell me that she had just tried to cash a check at the store and they had declined her request. She was out of gas, she was out of food, and she didn't know what to do. She was at her wits end and felt all alone and in despair.

I looked up at her with love and said, "Well now you do, don't you? You have the money to get gas, and to get food. I want you to know that someone is watching over you. You are never alone, even when you feel you are."

As I left her side, I noticed something that she didn't have before.

She had hope in her eyes.

What a beautiful lesson that wonderful afternoon brought all of us.

Sometimes we are the answer to someone else's prayers. In that service of love, we receive as much as the other person does.

I have felt that same feeling as that beautiful girl did. I think most of us have felt that alone, that forgotten, that destitute.

But we are not, and when we reach up for help and understanding, we will always receive answers, help, comfort, and support.

No matter what.

Points to ponder:

- Prayer doesn't have to be uttered in a certain order; you simply need to have an intention to connect and open your heart.

- Allow the answers and requests to show up in whatever manner they do; the expectation of where they will come from is what convinces us that we don't get answers from prayers. The answers will show up.

- For big decisions, I will sometimes request that my answer come in the form of something visual that I will see. In that manner, I won't ever second guess it. Many times for me it is in the form of a butterfly.

- You are often the answer to someone else's prayers. Be open to the gentle nudges and take action.

- You can ask for assistance with anything. You aren't being a bother—ask for help and be specific in your requests. I will sometimes ask for an angel specializing in travel arrangements to help me find the perfect itinerary for a trip. They are there; utilize their goodness and grace, and then thank them

Chapter 10
TRUTH ABOUT RELATIONSHIPS

I tried to quiet my grumbling tummy as I sat in the padded seats surrounded by women in my church. I was very intentional that day and had a great purpose for fasting and praying and being in that building on that beautiful spring day.

It was Fast Sunday. In my church, this is a day held once per month to separate yourself from the cravings of this world so you can commune more closely with God. I also believed that it put me in a holier position to receive answers and prove to God that I was a loving daughter of His, that I was obedient and would sacrifice my own desire for food and water in order to be with Him. That day I yearned for only one thing. I yearned that my husband of twenty years would finally come back to church with me.

Sunday after Sunday I would watch other families come into the building hand-in-hand with their significant others and the littles in tow. I, however, would stumble into church (usually late) with one of the kids that I had begged, bargained with, and berated for hours to come with me so that they could learn how to be with God.

I was in my third-hour class, which consisted of only women. I don't believe I heard a word from the teacher because I was engrossed in my mission to save my husband. I just knew that if his heart was softened, he would return to God and that we would become a happy little family once again. I didn't understand why I was always the one "doing" and "working," and why he seemed to float through life not caring one bit or taking this earthly life seriously.

I mean, didn't he realize it wasn't just about him? He had responsibilities and commitments and stewardship over these tiny humans he chose to bring into the world!

Finally, the meetings were over and I started to gather my belongings. The woman sitting next to me sighed, cleared her throat, and said, "I am not sure why I am supposed to say this to you, but I learned long ago not to question this voice and just do as it says. Are you searching for some answers today? Are you fasting and praying?"

"Yes, I am. I am pleading with the Lord to help my family," I declared. I was so excited, I thought I would jump out of my seat! Here it goes; here is the miracle I had been waiting for.

"The Lord says . . . Love him where he's at."

What . . . the . . . freak?!

I was pissed. My intentions were honorable. I wanted a family that was forever, not just now. I wanted to worship together. I wanted to pray together. I wanted to read scriptures together. This would make my Heavenly Father happy, and if I obeyed, I knew it would make me happy too!

Why would God say that?

Doesn't He want to help me create the recipe I was taught?

I mean, it wasn't like I was asking for a million dollars or a Mercedes-Benz, right?

These were good things to yearn for—eternal salvation things. If my husband didn't get on board with the program, we wouldn't be able to live together forever. Wasn't that worth fighting for?

And why wasn't God helping me to do the very thing He requires of me to live with Him once again?

Even my prayers and fasting and sacrifice weren't enough, it seemed. All the doing and grieving and suffering . . . wasn't God listening? Didn't He understand my heart and see my desire to be a good daughter of God?

And quite honestly, each time I would get a God "download" of truth, initially I would reject it and feel like I was being punished when in reality, these five words would change everything for me in terms of my marriage.

Love him where he is at. Isn't that what we all desire?

For someone to see us, understand us, and value us without any changes? Isn't that what unconditional love is and what Christ emulated during His time on this Earth?

My ego said I knew it all, that I had the magic recipe that would allow us to have everything I felt was missing. I knew the answer, and he didn't. If only he would help me more around the house; if only he would take care of the children more; if only he would make more money; if only he would be less frivolous with the money we had; if only he would treat me with respect and speak kindly to me. If only.

Most of us think that we can fill a missing piece with another person's love, that we cannot be complete or whole without a significant other filling in the gaps of what we don't believe is enough. And the expectations are stifling and suffocating. It was my husband's job to make me complete, whole, and happy. He needed to follow the exact formula that I laid out in order for that to happen.

And yet, the most loving thing we can do is step back and see that another person is navigating this journey we call life, just like we are. If we step back far enough, we can value the person they *are* without the expectations of what they need to *do* in order to be valued or deserve the love that we guard so carefully within our own hearts.

One chooses fear. We fear that if *they* don't do certain things, *we* aren't doing life right. What does doing life right mean, anyways? There are seven billion people on this planet. Aren't we all "doing life" in a slightly different way? What if we were to support and love and cheer on our mates, instead of requiring that they see things with our lenses?

What this statement meant to me was to step back and allow him room to grow, to fall, to experience life on his own terms, while I fully stepped into my life.

And that is when I took 100% responsibility for my own happiness, for my own earthly experience. I could choose to love, to go to church, and to worship in the way that I found delightful, and he could worship in his own way, or not at all.

That single shift in perspective changed everything. He no longer felt trapped or coerced to do things his spirit wasn't yearning for. He felt my love regardless of his actions and it allowed him to step more fully into his own power.

How many times do we choose fear in relationships? How often do we want to control outcomes by forcing our personal opinions on those we love the most?

I remember forcing my oldest child to go to church every week. If he didn't go, he would lose all entertainment privileges for the following week. Week after week, he proved to me that I was indeed not in control and that he was a sovereign individual who, at the ripe age of ten, could tell me to "go to hell," more or less.

In reality, what was I teaching him? That going to church would magically open a portal to communing with God? What if I instead could have chosen love, and sat with him on the couch and asked how he feels and hears God? Would that have had a different outcome?

Absolutely. He would have felt loved and valued and my beautiful boy of ten years old would have learned how to communicate on his own terms and in his own way. Basically, all I taught him through fear was to resent all religions and to associate church with being held hostage.

But we do this all the time, don't we? I see so many mothers running their little ones to every experience imaginable—dance, soccer, piano—and forcing them to take AP classes, all of which is showing them that life is all about proving your worth by what you do. The mothers are left exhausted and unappreciated, and the children are taught to be in constant motion, and that being quiet is lazy and unproductive. We must be productive. We must do everything we can to become the person we are supposed to be.

And guess what? They will never feel like they are enough. They will never do enough to earn approval from themselves. They must do more, have more, become more. And one day, they will self-implode because their spirit will no longer tolerate the madness.

And the worry that we feel is palpable. We spend countless nights worrying about our loved ones and believing that this worry is because we love so much. I have heard from my own mother and many others that, "being a mother means we get to worry."

I recently took this question to God, and He laid out worry on the table for me. I saw that at the root of worry is the energy of control and mistrust—not trusting that the person that we are worrying about has the ability to navigate this life and do it right. We feel uptight because we need to come up with some answers because it is up to us to save the day. And of course, also at the root is pervasive fear. And when we are in fear, we are far from the love that we state that this worry comes from.

I then asked what could replace this worry I was so familiar with. Again, I was shown that we can choose to be the greatest cheerleader, best advocate, and be willing to allow another individual to use their agency to experience life in the manner that will teach them the best. It is loving to sit on the sidelines and cheer. Also running out on the field if someone needs a quick dusting off and help to get back on their feet, but then running back to the stands, is the loving action of kindness that awaits us on the sidelines.

Moms and dads, let's be blatantly honest here. We do it because we are so freaking scared—scared that we will get it all wrong. That the two decades we get to raise a child will not be enough time. That we mess it up and that they will end up feeling like we do: inadequate, forlorn, and discouraged with life. That all the things that everyone *says* will make us happy, will never be enough.

Let's also talk about ourselves as parents, as spouses, and as sons or daughters. So often we do things in order to get a reaction—any reaction, or any love at all—in exchange for what we did. And when we don't get it, we hold resentment like it is a prized possession, never allowing it to leave our clutches for fear we will not have gained anything at all for sacrificing ourselves on the altar of life.

I don't know about other mothers out there, but my experience as a mother was lived through other people. I felt strongly that I should have no desire to do anything for myself. Every ounce of my energy was to be poured into others and to be lived through other people's successes and failures. And if my children were unhappy, I was unhappy. If my children were experiencing accolades from the world, so was I.

I can vividly recall walking through the door many times after a very long day at work. My husband and kids would be watching another episode of *SpongeBob* and asking in very whiny voices," What's for dinner? I'm so hungry!"

I would go through the pantry and refrigerator to find ingredients to make something, anything, that would hopefully appeal to those that I loved so desperately. After the meal was gobbled up, I would promptly go straight to washing the dishes, then getting the kids into baths, and then tucking them into the safety of their own beds.

And . . . I was pissed.

I was so incredibly resentful of those I loved the most.

Why wouldn't my husband know that I needed his help? That I was so tired?

Why wouldn't my kids help more, do more, be more respectful?

And then the statement, "love them where they are at," started to take form and shape in my life. It took several years—almost a decade—to truly become who I wanted to be in the way I show up in my relationship.

This statement wasn't simply for my loved ones. This statement was for me as well.

Love me where I'm at.

Could I do that?

It felt so foreign, so unfamiliar. I knew there were still things I needed to do in order to prove my worth.

But my soul saw the love in that statement, instead of the fear.

Love myself where I'm at.

What would that mean for my type A personality? The one that could strive and achieve goals like a boss. The one that could create and achieve every one of those vision board images. The one that was exhausted all the time. The one that *forced* herself to do things now that she was too tired. The one that felt hopeless much of the time because all the "things" that I was told would bring me happiness were not providing any happiness at all.

Would that mean I would just remain stagnant? Would that mean that my family wouldn't progress in this lifetime?

The fact of the matter is that if I wanted to stay on this earth, it meant that I had to start loving me, taking care of me, and treating myself with ultimate respect and love. No more self-betrayal. No more excuses for why I was last on the list. And no more false expectations that the things I do would provide the validation of my worth.

Love myself where I'm at.

I couldn't even remember what I liked anymore. What do I like to eat, what do I like to do for fun? What is fun?

Slowly, ever so slowly, I started to remember. I love yoga, hiking, and speaking. I love deep conversations about things that matter to me. Usually, those things are deep, spiritual conversations about my soul and others on their spiritual journey. I love all the hippy things. I love butterflies and hummingbirds. Did you know that hummingbirds are a symbol for finding joy?

I was starting to discover love and joy again. I learned that my favorite thing in the whole world was laughing. So, I found every opportunity to laugh again. I spent time with girlfriends and remembered that my happiness was important too. In fact, it was so important that if I chose to invest in everyone else but me, my spirit would die. I had to keep my soul alive in order to invest in anyone else.

I love dancing. I love dancing with my husband. I love dancing for him as I pass him in the hallways, because it makes him laugh and it makes me feel alive.

I started to remember what it was like to be alive again.

I was living. I was breathing. I was loving. I was embracing all the goodness in life.

And it wasn't because someone else was happy. I was happy.

I saw my husband start to come alive too. There is nothing more empowering for a man than to see his wife alive and happy. In his mind, he is doing something right. He is the protector in the family, so if I am thriving, it gives him permission to thrive as well. Yes, it is possible for them to do this without this validation. But it is easier when the ground is fertile with the right ingredients to step into joy.

Over a decade has passed since this statement was divinely given to me.

I think about my current relationship with my husband. How my husband loves to be with me. How he goes grocery shopping and cooks dinner without being asked. How he delights in buying me gifts to simply see my face light up. How he goes to silly galas and dresses up in kilts because I delight in knowing what is underneath. How I love making love, and connecting and living and breathing and being alive.

I am alive again.

As for my children: They see a mother who finds time for herself, who is glowing with a knowing that I am important, that my existence matters, and that I am fully embracing this discovery and journey we call life.

And this gives them a better blueprint for their own lives.

I am sure all mothers can relate, that we all say," I just want my children to be happy."

How can your children be happy if you don't know how to be happy?

We can't give them the recipe unless we find it ourselves. Is it possible that you have forgotten? Is it possible that you could find it once again?

Is it possible for you to live once again?

Can you choose you this time?

Points to Ponder:

- Do one thing today that makes you feel good. Dance like nobody's watching. Laugh at something you would normally get upset over—honestly, most things don't need to be serious. Humans are so funny when you watch the craziness unfolding before you. Laughing can make you feel alive again.

- Go for a walk without anyone else. Look at the beauty around you.

- Next time someone does something that upsets you, ask God, "What is another way of looking at this? What more is there?" (This last question is something I learned from my dear mentor Angel Lyn).

- Today, focus on you and your healing. Anytime you wish someone else would change so you would feel better, show up for yourself and choose to shift perspective and know that you are always in control of how you feel, no matter what is happening.

- Find out more about you today. What do you love? What do you dislike? Start to notice what sets your heart on fire and do more of that.

- When you start to worry about someone, catch yourself and decide to shift that energy into one of a cheerleader and believe that the person can and will choose the best option for their growth and development—you simply need to get out of the way and send love instead of fear.

Chapter 11

TRUTH ABOUT RELIGION

I was hiking through the hills that I have fallen in love with. The red rocks and red sand in contrast to the bluest skies sing to my soul and call me to walk amid Mother Earth. It is here that I always find peace among the chaos and feel like I am home once again.

As I was hiking, I heard the gentle words, "Are you going to trust me?"

What an interesting question. Wait, I thought . . . I believe I do trust you, God.

And then I said out loud, "God, I believe my actions speak louder than my words, and I have done some things in the last few years that have been directly for you; what do you mean 'trust you?'" I replied. And then I thought about the countless hours I'd spent organizing and collaborating to put on the largest women's interfaith conference ever held in the state of Utah.

Three months prior, I had also been asked to serve as the Young Women's president in my congregation in the Church of Jesus Christ of Latter-day Saints. This is one of the most time-intensive volunteer assignments you can undertake in the Church. It requires coordinating with seven other women who are also helping to lead the eleven- to eighteen-year-old girls. Assignments include weekly activities, bi-weekly Sunday lessons, multiple awards nights, extra firesides (special presentations), weekly leadership planning meetings, and planning and carrying out both an annual girls camp and an annual youth conference. I was told that the bishop had been inspired to ask me to lead in this capacity, and it was considered a privilege and honor to work with the highest priority in the church—the youth.

So, why did my body completely freeze and lock from my chest up moments after I had been asked to serve? It felt as though a demon was standing behind me and putting their claws into my shoulders and rib cage. I couldn't breathe, relax, or stop the constant anxiety coursing through my body. For quite a while, I tried every tool in my box to calm my nervous system: breathing, meditating, using essential oils, engaging in energy work, receiving massage, and using CBD oils. And yet my nervous system would not calm down. It took almost six weeks before the anxiety left my system and allowed me to relax and receive once again.

I had just finished putting on the Young Women's camp. In reality, it was a Young Women's retreat. After the 2020 pandemic, I felt the young women didn't really know each other anymore. So I pleaded the case with my bishop and convinced him that the girls needed pampering and connection. I loved watching the girls as they started to remember who they were. I basked in the goodness of witnessing the shift in perspective and self-love that occurs when we finally embrace our wholeness rather than our perceived brokenness.

But there was such a disconnect between myself and the calling this time. I found myself reading the lessons and screaming inside, "NO, I cannot teach this!!!" Why, I wondered, had Satan gotten a hold of me and started quietly binding me with cords like I had been taught he could do? Why did I bathe in the goodness of peace and tranquility when I studied scriptures or other books of God, like *A Course in Miracles*, or *Love without Conditions?* Or when I simply sat in my own divinity, quietly observing the magnificence of this life? Or when I walked in the red hills of southern Utah?

And yet, when I walked into the church building, why was it that all I felt was fear?

There was a part of me screaming that I needed to get the recipe right. If I went to the temple more, if I fasted more, if I prayed more, if I studied approved church materials more, maybe I would finally figure out why everyone else said that this was the only true gospel of Jesus Christ. And if I could get it right, I would feel a peace like nothing else could provide. That was what I was told my whole life. Get the recipe right, and you will feel happy.

And yet, I didn't.

I felt pressure. I felt this need to judge others to see if anyone out there was getting it right. I felt that, if there was someone out there living this existence that they spoke about in church and was finally "there" in that peace and tranquility, then maybe if I tried harder, I could be "there" too.

But the other part of my being kept calling to me and reminding me that I had been having these thoughts of disconnection for four years. During the years of the interfaith conference, I met women from all different faiths varying from non-denominational Christian, to Buddhism, Catholicism, Muslim, Baptist, and those who called themselves spiritual and not religious. So many of these women displayed such reverence and confidence in their salvation and I saw and felt that they were aligned and connected with God. They didn't seem to be fearful. In fact, they seemed to be free from the worry of having to do something to receive God's love. And what I noticed was that, when they were in that space of love, they radiated that love outward because they embodied love.

One Sunday, the lesson I was to teach was about avoiding pornography. I had just recently had the experience of having my sexual awakening at fifty years of age, and my spirit screamed, "Why don't we talk about the gloriousness of sex?!" These girls deserved to know the power of their sexuality and not the constant discussion of ignoring that part of our lives. Why was the lesson always about what you should NOT do, but never about doing what your spirit would delight in doing because it honors and respects your being?

I chose to talk about pornography for about two minutes and then started a discussion about why so many individuals are fearful of talking about sex. I encouraged them to consider how detrimental this thinking is when you consider that this is the very way we were created. So, as my friend Laurel Huston says, "If sex is a subject that is 'dirty,' what does that make us if we were created through sex?"

The girls were eager to delve into something they had been feeling about what had been happening inside them, and were relieved to be given permission to discuss it in a healthy way. I could see the layers of guilt and shame slough off of them as they realized that they weren't broken and that, in fact, they were experiencing the feeling of energy and one of God's greatest gifts.

This discussion was met with some discomfort by many others. I understand and love the members of my congregation, and I know that all of us were taught to respect sex as belonging within the confines of marriage. Yet there was never ever any discussion on the power of sex that allows two people to create, and their power to align together with Source Energy. There is nothing in this lifetime that is more powerful. I believe as a society we have been missing the mark on this one.

Along with the discussion on sex, there were several other lessons I simply couldn't even teach and I would gently hand them off either to one of the girls or to another leader. Any lesson that taught that the girls needed to go to certain individuals for insight and knowledge left me sick to my stomach, because I knew that they had all of the answers within them. I believe that others around us can provide considerations and insight that can help us understand things more clearly, but the goal is to learn to listen and hear directly from within.

During my time spent with the girls and the women, my only goal was to help them remember. I aimed to help them to discover their true essence and to fall in love, one step at a time, with the girl inside—the girl who was never broken, never flawed—who is a divine being having a human experience.

But I couldn't do it anymore. I felt like a complete fraud walking through those doors each week. It wasn't who I was at the core of my being, and so when I heard the voice, "Are you going to trust me?" I knew I had been worshiping the acceptance of man instead of worshiping the God that I love.

"Yes, I will," I actually said out loud. "What does that look like and what does that mean?"

"You don't need to know what it looks like. Simply follow me and I will show you," God said.

The church manual wasn't going to be a blueprint anymore. God was asking me to trust the voice inside, the voice that I had betrayed over and over throughout my life. I was being asked to trust her, to fall in love with her, and in exchange, I would discover the "more" I had been searching for all of my life. The thing was, this "more" was a façade. It had always been there and had never changed— only my perspective had changed.

A month later, I heard the voice encourage me to turn in my keys to the bishop. A Young Women's president is given a set of keys to the church building. Very few individuals had these keys and it was considered a true privilege to have them.

I knew what this meant. This meant I was done. It was official— I was stepping into my new phase of trusting myself and shifting away from needing a blueprint on how to get there. I felt as if I were walking off a cliff and trusting that God would catch me.

I asked God for a sign. This was BIG for me. This was potentially the biggest decision I had ever made because I had been taught since birth that if I didn't follow this system, I would pay for it with my eternal salvation.

This is a very hefty price, and one I didn't want to get wrong.

"God, please show me a large, yellow and black butterfly if this is what you are encouraging me to do. I want to ensure that my mind is not playing tricks on me, so please help me make the best decision possible. I ask that you provide this sign prior to my meeting with the bishop today. I will find trust and faith in either answer. If I do not see the butterfly, I will continue to serve in this capacity as a Young Women's leader and place all thoughts of doubt on the altar."

The meeting was to take place an hour after church ended. I drove home and sat on my back porch with my journal and pen, writing down thoughts and pondering on the questions of my heart. I started to get up from my chair to go to the meeting when the largest butterfly I had ever seen slowly, ever so slowly, flew in front of me. I had some AirPods in my ears and some beautiful instrumental music playing while I journaled and as I went to turn it off, I noticed that the song was called, "Butterflies."

Jaw.Dropped.

My adrenaline started pumping as I approached the church building because I *knew* what I was going to do.

I asked for strength, and used a voice of confidence in talking to this bishop that I loved. He was a good man, doing the best that he could. All of the members were good people doing the best they could. I love them. I love their hearts, I love their serving spirits. I love the smell of the building. I love the sound of the hymns. I love the sacrament.

But I love God more. I love Jesus Christ more. I love my Heavenly Mother more.

The bishop kindly asked me why. He explained that he felt like I had a deep connection to God—why would I leave if I had a testimony of God and Jesus Christ?

We discussed my love for them, and that everything in my life revolved around this relationship. Nothing was more important. Everything I do is because of my love for God and myself and others. Because we are all one with God.

He asked me about my testimony of the priesthood and I explained that I had one, but it differed from the definition that the church outlined. He asked me about my testimony of the leaders of the church. I said that I believed they were good men and women and that the messages were based on peace and love. All of those things I resonate with deeply.

His last question was, "Do you sustain the Prophet of God and will you follow his guidance and direction?" ("prophet" in this question refers to the Prophet of the Church of Jesus Christ of Latter-day Saints).

I replied, "I will follow him provided my own intuition is consistent with what he says. However, if my own personal revelation is different, I will follow that EVERY SINGLE TIME. I will follow God above man."

That was when he said, "Let's decide to agree to disagree on that one."

"Okay bishop . . . Here are the keys."

I drove home and cried. I cried in grief for the things that I would be "losing" in order to gain more. I cried for the relationships that would change because of this decision. I cried because I was damn proud of myself for doing one of the hardest things I have ever done.

I was finally not betraying myself, and was honoring the voice inside.

I was finally free and ready to expand on a new level of remembering.

This chapter is not about discounting or making the claim that religion is false. Rather, it is a chapter about the absolute, unconditional love that God has for us and that because of this love, He will speak to us in the language of our heart.

I have no anger toward my religion of origin. I love the people, the buildings, the leaders, the teachers, and the customs. They feel familiar to me. I love the beauty and familiarity of the building as I walk in. I love the people as they all serve in various capacities in the Church, giving of their time and talents. These halls have become safe for them. They love the guidance and the rules and the structure of a religious organization. And the principles of love and service will always allow us to feel the divine source of love that we all have access to.

But for me, the halls started to become a box— a box from inside of which I started to see the top open slightly, and my naturally curious nature wanted to peek out. Once I peeked, I noticed truth and love in so many places outside of the familiar confines of my original beliefs and understanding.

I saw the truth in *A Course in Miracles*. I opened the pages and the first line stated, "This is a book of peace." As I read the sometimes-confusing messages in this book, I saw myself changing on a deeper level. The principles were easy but also very complex. Through the years of programming and self-interpretation, I had come to look upon the world with my own perception and judgments, fears and biases.

This book started to shift me back to my truth. I started understanding that my thoughts of inferiority and suffering were of my own making. This is both a beautiful thing to recognize and a tough thing to swallow at the same time. It is empowering because

I can choose to stop creating chaos in my life, but at the same time I understand that I create the pain in my own life. It was sobering, and also enlightening and wonderful.

I now see truth and wonder and beauty in everything around me. I notice the colors and the textures and wonder of nature. I feel my Mother Earth's love as I wander through dirt paths, and hear the synchronicity of the natural rhythm of life, and see the interconnected beings we all are. I see the light in a stranger's eyes and know that we "know each other" but have simply forgotten.

Is it possible I could have had these same feelings in the faith of my origin? Possibly. I know many individuals who seem to find in that religion the love and beauty I have described. But for me, I couldn't fathom that there was only one way back to God.

An unconditionally loving being would be just that, unconditional. There are no conditions, there are no singular paths back to the love of my God. It is always with me; it is always swirling in my heart and if I open it, I can feel it pulsing throughout my being. I don't need to do anything to feel it. In fact, the less I do, the more I feel. The distractions surrounding us most often lead us away from that voice, and it is quieting the mind so the soul can speak that will take us back home to ourselves.

Freedom is found in finding that love.

Freedom is found in finding our own love.

It is possible, and even powerful, to find our own religion in our own heart. The blueprint of our soul is found within and not without.

At the core of this inner religion is love.

We will either be in love or fear. Period.

I once had a discussion with someone who felt fear about the fact that I was being guided by my inner compass rather than listening to the external voices or religion telling me how and why and when. In their perspective, the only way to actually know the path was to follow a singular way of thinking, and that there is only one way. I could feel their fear that I was walking off of a cliff and that they would no longer have me with them in the afterlife.

I have compassion for this thought. When you love someone, it can be new territory when they veer off a path you don't know, especially if you have been taught that this path was the only way.

We talked about fear and love. This person stopped me for a minute and said, "I don't fear . . . I don't fear death; I welcome it!"

My response: "I know you don't fear death, but is it possible that you fear life?"

I believe the greatest lesson in this story will help others understand that they are free. When they follow their heart, it won't necessarily be easy. Telling my mother was the hardest thing I've ever done, but I felt impressed that if I didn't share my truth, she wouldn't have the experience of learning unconditional love.

By staying in the dark, I was keeping her in the dark as well. The most loving thing we can do is live our truth because doing so allows others the learning and growth they deserve.

So be brave.

Do the hard.

Live your truth.

Set yourself free.

What if this life consists of us creating heaven or hell? What if in each moment we can choose to feel glorious and peaceful and grounded and centered, or we can choose to feel less than enough, short of the goals in front of us, and somehow flawed?

What if the very thing we have been searching for never left us for even a second?

What if we simply left it?

I feel the surge of gathering where we are starting to walk away from the madness and return back to our own inner sanctuary. The external world has become so chaotic that we are being brought to our knees in pursuit of comfort and solace.

We are being led home. The Christ Consciousness is expanding and radiating from our own inner beings. And . . . it is glorious to watch. Instead of watching the madness on the news, start watching what is happening to your own awareness and the shifts that are happening in others.

Awareness is the beginning . . . it's time to return home, my friends.

The peace you seek is closer than you think.

I now invite you to define what is right in your heart. Are you following the customs that you were raised in? Does that feel peaceful and glorious, or does it feel heavy and have fear attached to it? I encourage you to pay close attention to your feelings as you study and ponder and pray. Are you aligning with God in the manner that is right for you, or are you employing a manner that someone told you is the only way?

Love is all-inclusive. Love is light- and peace-driven. If it is exclusive and has parameters on receiving all that is in store for you—question it. Be brave enough to honor your soul and consider that there may be more, or perhaps you may be incorrectly interpreting what you have been taught. Maybe the blame and shame you have sat in your whole life doesn't allow for the love to filter through to you.

This faith transition was one of the most challenging things I have ever encountered. Since it is believed that this decision will have negative everlasting consequences, the fear is felt at an intense level. I started to notice this fear that pervaded so much of the culture in my faith tradition. When I shifted into love, I learned that my life was a series of experiences. I still had a right to choose painful and glorious experiences based on what I put out, but my final destination would never be impacted.

My perception of scripture even changed. The Ten Commandments morphed into the ten commitments. A loving God that gave us free agency wouldn't command us to do anything. Rather, with a change of heart and a commitment to love, those things naturally occur. For instance, when I am aligned with God, I have no need to commit murder, because I love

humanity too much and realize we are all connected. When I am aligned with God, I don't covet other people or their things or want to steal, because things become so trivial in the big picture. It isn't a to do list when it is a commitment—it is a way of being.

In his book, *Conversations with God: An Uncommon Dialogue*, Neale Donald Walsch wrote:

"There is no such thing as 'getting into heaven.' There is only knowing that you are already there.

"The irony is that most people think that they have to leave where they are to get where they need to be. And so, they leave heaven in order to get to heaven, and go through hell.

"Enlightenment is understanding that there is nowhere to go, nothing to do, and nobody you need to be except exactly who you're being right now."

Doesn't that statement feel light? When I read it, it feels expansive and I know that truth resides in it. My heart yearned for this for so long. It knew that there weren't any hoops to jump through or a to-do list of proving our worth.

Just being is enough.

Just remembering is enough.

Love is always enough.

Points to Ponder:

- As you read spiritual materials, what feels light and expansive? What seems confusing and dark? My suggestion is to stick with the expansive materials and to rely on those as sources that speak the language of your heart.

- Remember a time when you felt love. Sit in meditation for at least five minutes and feel that love radiate through your body. Come back to this as often as you need it. Love is always available when we ask and focus.

- Ask for assistance through prayer, meditation, or a question asked out loud as to what the next step will be to discover your truth. Listen for the answer and take action on that next step. The right book, teacher, and idea will be revealed and you will be led back home with each step you take.

Chapter 12
TRUTH ABOUT MONEY

It had been quite a day. I had just taught my third essential-oil class in one day, and was looking forward to relaxing and taking it easy. My phone rang. I looked at the caller ID, noticing it was my sweet husband. I love that he has a desire to talk to me often. During this time, my entire family was making a significant sacrifice. I had taken the greatest risk of my entire life up until that point.

I had quit my stable job of thirteen years with the Utah Foster Care Foundation in order to pursue my dream of becoming an entrepreneur and teaching others the power of essential oils.

It was exhilarating and scary and exciting and daring. But I took the plunge. I knew it was time to branch out when I had my last employee review. My exact job description outlined the basic tasks for my position. Find, recruit, and screen potential foster parents for the counties that I represented. I loved it, and over the years I had come to find new, innovative ways to find foster parents. That was the part of the job I loved the most. And these programs were now used statewide as best practices, helping to gather families in unprecedented numbers. And I was proud of that accomplishment.

In this review, my newly appointed supervisor started by saying, "Wendy, we have a love/hate relationship with all of the extra things you do in your position here."

What? Confused, I asked, "What do you mean, you 'hate'?"

He explained that while they appreciated all of the things that we did within my office, these things weren't expected and they may have a negative impact on the others that shared the same job title within the organization. He asked me to stick closer to my job description so that everyone would be doing the same things, which would ultimately make everyone feel more comfortable.

Astonished, I replied, "So, you are asking me to stop doing additional things that benefit children in the state of Utah, so that others might feel more comfortable?"

With that knowledge, I knew immediately that my part-time gig would step into the forefront and replace my full-time career. I was tired of playing small in life overall. With the government mentality of doing only the minimum in order for them to not have to raise the bar the following year, I knew in my heart that I was destined to do more, be more, and have more.

So, I turned in my notice and cashed out my 401K in order to support my share of bills until I could be consistent with the income from my business.

And here I was in Oklahoma City, standing next to a pool after teaching classes for hours about one of the things that I love so much in this world: essential oils. I remember opening a bottle for the first time. I had a physical response immediately upon opening it up. And that was all it took for me to be hooked. I used oils for just about everything: fighting physical ailments, first aid, cooking, cleaning, and emotional and mental support. And my business was soaring. I was creating the life of my dreams with something I adore and a company I believed in.

But I heard my husband on the other line and he was noticeably shaken.

"Dan, what's going on?"

"Wendy, I was fired today."

What? My husband held one of the most stable jobs on the planet as a police officer for a small-town department. How in the world could he just be let go? He had earned the officer of the year award, two lifesaving awards . . . and yet he was fired?

I remember sitting in my hotel room that night and fear creeping over my body like a heavy blanket of darkness. I don't think I breathed much that evening. It was suffocating, and every part of my being was screaming as I realized that I was now 100% responsible for the financial stability of my family. And I wasn't ready. I didn't want that responsibility, and I wrestled with the demons in my head as they tried to overtake me again and again and again.

The next day as I showed up at another class, I felt desperate. I wasn't sharing what I loved anymore. I was begging and pleading inside that someone, anyone, would buy a bottle so that I could simply put food on the table and pay my bills. And . . . no one bought. I didn't sell even one single bottle.

From that point forward, the joy of teaching and loving something that brought me so many blessings had become a heavy burden. My safety and stability were completely shaken and here I was left wondering how I was going to support my family and also be an emotional support to my husband, who was crushed by the realization that he no longer was a part of something that he believed was his entire identity.

And my business tanked.

My once thriving business was sinking quickly and dissipating into thin air. I worked harder than I had ever worked before in my entire life. I taught classes, I rented booths at craft fairs, and I had a list of leads that I consistently called. I followed up with current clients and manipulated my way into having conversations about them joining me in this business.

But honestly, why would they? Why would someone buy something or join me in a business filled with fear, scarcity, and heaviness. I was far from inspiring, excited, and joyful like I was at the beginning. And just like that, the dream was morphing into a nightmare.

This story unfolds into a place where our family was forced into selling our beloved home, moving, and getting food stamps. It got much worse before it got better. But it did get better—a lot better—and I learned some natural laws around abundance and, more specifically, money.

I now enjoy the blessings of financial abundance and am eternally grateful for the lessons that the years of scarcity taught me about the overflow of all that is good, including money.

I love teaching about money because the subject of money ignites fear in a way that very few other things in our lives have power to ignite. Our very existence (or so we think) relies on us earning a living to provide for the basic needs of our families. And according to Maslow's hierarchy of needs, it is incredibly challenging to focus on self-realization when we have a hungry belly and have to worry about the safety of our children

But once you understand the laws of abundance, it is slightly easier to get back into the tasks that will bring abundance into your life. So many individuals believe that it takes money to make money, and while that is true to a point, I believe it is more likely that these individuals have a basic knowledge of financial flow and expect that it will always flow into their lives.

Let's start with the main basic truth:

Money is energy.

Period.

I would invite you to see how the story above ebbs and flows with the energy behind each stage of my financial situation. At the beginning, there was excitement and energy and natural drive stemming from a joy in sharing and being with others, teaching about something I loved. This high energy, or vibration, was magnetizing and drew in people who wanted to hear about oils. I naturally built my business on my positive attitude and excitement for this new-found knowledge. At this stage, my business flowed and was easier, allowing for things to flow into my life.

When I received the phone call that fateful night, I had one of two choices. I could have found peace within myself and a new excitement for my business. This situation could have catapulted me to the next level. Or, I could have succumbed to fear.

However, we know how the story goes; I succumbed to fear. That night in the hotel I felt fear buzzing through every cell of my being. This new vibration repelled money from me, and in essence built up a dam to prevent me from receiving. Even with constant work, and focused phone calls, my energy drove everything away from me.

During that time, I watched my husband shrink into a shell of what he once was. I was grieving the loss of the strength from my partner, along with feeling enormous pressure to produce. These two ingredients did not create a successful life.

I have since built a successful entrepreneurial career bringing in multiple six figures for my family, and I work significantly less than I used to.

We have material things that I once thought were only for the elect few, but which we now possess and enjoy. I travel the world and meet new people, learn about new cultures, and experience this world in a brand new way.

It was not my work ethic that changed; it was some basic rules that I learned that created a complete shift in perspective and thus allowed money flow to my family.

The first thing I learned was to change my vibration, or energy, so that things were naturally attracted into my life.

I am certain one of the first questions you may ask is . . . how?

You may also be someone who is lying in bed at night wondering how in the world you will pay your bills this month, and figuring out how to balance your checkbook and still have money left over for food.

I've been there. And I know the torture it creates and the fear that it instills in your heart.

But that feeling of fear is the thing that is driving away the very thing you desire. You desire safety, and peace of mind, and reaching goals, and providing a beautiful life for your family.

But there is a different way to do things. And this way may be surprising to you, but it is magic. Seriously, it is pure magic.

Do anything that will allow you to raise your energy and bring light and joy back into your life.

So basically, one of ways to create money is to have fun. It is a powerful way to create abundance.

Seriously.

And I have a saying that goes like this: If it ain't fun, it ain't done.

However, if the word "fun" doesn't resonate with you, you may still understand what it feels like to feel good. That is what I am talking about. My "good" always includes fun, so that is what lights my fire.

When we find joy or happiness or laughter or fun, we shake this vibration up and allow things to start flowing again. And sometimes when our energy is very low, we need to learn how to change our vibration intentionally by having something we can turn to easily when we are not in creation mode and have the desire to be there. Money flows to this high vibrational energy.

Some ways to raise your vibrational energy may include:

- Turn on your favorite music and dance!
- Do something physical you enjoy, such as hiking, working out, practicing yoga, or running/walking.
- Make love.
- Have lunch with a positive friend (stay away from friends that give you permission to sit in your stuff and validate your victimization).
- Do something childish, like swing on a swing set, or spin in a circle.
- Watch a comedy on TV.
- Invite friends over for dinner.
- Play games with your family.

I have several realtor friends that complain that the moment they go on vacation, their business explodes with business. Now, this isn't always wanted during vacation mode, but it visually shows how this principle works. The reason they get busy is that they aren't focusing all of their energy on their business and they are shifting into an energy of excitement and anticipation. That excitement and happiness drives the energy of abundance.

I recently had a luxury co-listing with another agent who was going to Italy for two weeks. We had done a great job at marketing and getting the high-priced listing noticed by the public, but we didn't have any offers. The day before she left for this trip, we had several offers come in and I helped get the home under contract the day she left. Her excitement and high vibration energy brought the energy in for abundance and prosperity. Twenty days later we received a large paycheck from that transaction.

This doesn't mean you simply go have fun and that truckloads of money will show up. What it does mean is that you learn to use your time in the office wisely, and then focus on keeping your vibration high when you can feel things shift and your energy get lower. It is about being instead of doing.

There is a beautiful art you get to learn in terms of knowing what is highest and best for your business at any moment. Using the various techniques you learned in the intuition portion of this book, you will start to notice what is next for you on the to-do list. Our minds can only conceptualize so much in terms of tangible things we should do, so we learn and lean into the voice in our heart to know what is next.

I love what one of my dearest friends and mentors, Laurel Huston, calls this: "tuning in and turning on." You take a moment to listen to what your heart is telling you and then you take bold action immediately. Laurel also reminds us that our minds are a clock and our hearts are our compass. She once asked, "So why are we taking direction from a clock?" It is our hearts that will guide us to this creation that will bring us massive abundance in every area of our lives.

I would encourage you to read the intuition section of this book if you are confused or in distress over not hearing your heart. It will take practice and patience and compassion for yourself as you learn how to "tune in." And learning to be brave and take action every time is also going to allow you to grow and learn how to trust yourself again.

I get a lot of referrals from my brokerage for real estate clients in my area. Out of every ten referrals, I usually get two that truly have a desire to find a home in my community. I have become so good at listening to my heart that I will instinctively know which one to call right away. There is a rule of thumb that if you call these contacts back within ten minutes of receiving the lead, you will have a much greater chance of securing them as a client. The problem with this ten-minute rule is that there are other things that are commanding my attention throughout the day. That is why tuning in is so important. I look over the email, tune in, and if I feel that familiar expansion, I immediately call. If I don't, I will put their names aside and call when a more opportune time comes along.

I used this exact technique last summer when I took an entire month off from work to recalibrate my system and get some needed rest for a more prolonged time. One day as I was driving back from hiking, I noticed a referral that came through. I had several of these names come through during that month, but I "noticed" this one. I understood this gentle nudging so I immediately called. These clients were ready to purchase the home that they had already found online, and they wanted me to sell their current home as well. After I got off the phone, I handed them over to my colleague that I had hired when I took a month off, and got back to enjoying my vacation.

That is another story that deserves some time. Last summer, I was fast approaching burnout, and my body was screaming at me to stop. When you do not learn to listen and stop the doing, your body will often be the one to stop you in your tracks. As I lay in my bathtub one night, weary with exhaustion, I prayed out loud and said, "God, I am so incredibly tired and I don't know how to keep going."

The answer was . . . don't keep going.

So, I pondered that message. What does that mean? I then thought about how many Europeans would take a month or two off each year in order to relax and restore themselves.

Was this even possible? Was this a thing?

I didn't know, but the thought excited every cell of my body. So, I opened my mind up to it. What would it look like to take a month off? As I imagined it, I started to form ideas on how it could possibly take shape. A local agent popped into my mind. I respected and trusted her expertise and she had recently moved into the same area, so she was building her business and presence here locally.

This is where the action takes place—I called her. I asked if she would like to sit down and go over a business proposition that may benefit both of us. We went to lunch a few days later, and I explained that I had a desire to take an entire month off and turn off my phone because my body was pleading with me to slow down and relax again. We went over terms that would give her the ability to make some good extra money, allow my clients to still be served well, and allow me to continue benefiting from those relationships in time and money.

Last July was a time of some of my most prized memories. I went on three trips back-to-back. I discovered Oregon with my family, I traveled to Maui with my older daughter, and went on a river rafting trip with a bunch of youth.

And most individuals might think I took a dive in my business. But the law of energy and abundance loved the fact that I was having fun, honoring my body and resting, and loving my life. The following month, I had my highest grossing month to date.

Isn't that fabulous?

And the greatest part of this? Abundance is for all of us. There isn't a limit on what is available or possible. When I create massive wealth, it only visually shows you that you are capable of creating it too. My piece of the pie doesn't take away from yours. The pie simply gets bigger.

And when we all step into a place of abundance, we have more to give others. We have more time, energy, financial ability, and love to give to everyone else.

Money is a magnifier. If you are a good person, it magnifies your ability to do more for this world. If you are a bad person, it will give you power to do more evil in this world.

But let's be honest. If you are reading this book, it is because you have a desire to learn the truth and have a different life full of peace and love. You, my friend, are good. Money will expand this goodness inside of you.

My goal one day is to donate enough money to bring a program to my local area that serves individuals who were sexually violated before the age of eighteen. The week-long program that I took part in at the beginning of my healing was something I will never forget. It was located on a ten-acre estate with a Zen Pond, walking trails, and a river nearby. The home was this palatial, 10,000 square foot oasis. Between receiving instruction, individual and group therapy, healthy food, and yoga and tai chi classes, the stage was set for me to begin my own healing. I can vividly recall driving through the gates and into the sweeping driveway, recognizing that God had provided heaven and angels to surround me as I approached the bravest thing I had done up to that point.

In this way, the process of healing is extended to thousands more.

Do you see how having financial means can help the masses? Is it possible that with more financial stability, you could focus on others in a way that is difficult when you are concerned with how you will feed your family?

However, I do caution you with one thing in terms of money, and that is believing that money will erase all of your problems.

This couldn't be further from the truth. Money expands everything. This energy will also expand your awareness and allow you the time to stare in the face of the monsters you previously didn't want to see, or were too busy worrying about money to notice. If you step into this stage and aren't ready to face your demons and do the work to shed old beliefs and old patterns, and to forgive yourself and others, you may find that this void of worrying fills up with boredom, loneliness, and unfulfillment.

So many people reach all of their goals, only to feel lonelier at the top than they did at the bottom. Remember that we will never ever feel fulfillment from external sources. Those who aren't ready will continue searching outside of themselves. They will wonder why money didn't give them the continual peace and joy that they were seeking, so they start to look at things like sex, power, and substances to numb the pain.

External sources are simply tools we can use to create. And in that context, you will be able to use this tool of money to create massive amounts of good in this world. The peace and joy and satisfaction will come from using this tool to expand your spiritual gifts and show up in this world unapologetically as yourself. Utilizing these gifts for the greater good of man will be a healing balm for your soul.

The most important thing I have yet to share is that you won't receive these additional resources unless you believe you deserve them.

"What? Of course I deserve them," you may say.

Don't believe me? Look over the statistics of individuals who have won the lottery and how many end up in the same financial boat that they were in (usually worse off) a year or two later. This is because they didn't believe that they were worthy of such wealth.

They will make poor decisions with money and seem to throw it away because they believe that they, themselves, are trash.

And so off it goes . . . into thin air.

Changing those beliefs and learning to love and respect yourself will start to shift those things ever so gently during your journey. And usually, it progresses in stages. The healthiest way to accumulate wealth is to learn how to accept it a little more at a time. Gaining wealth quickly can be detrimental to the stages of learning how to receive and to how to heal wounds and old beliefs along the way.

I recall realizing, not that long ago, that I wanted a new car. I had the resources and started looking at the regular makes and models that I would normally look at. As I started to get serious, I noticed that many of the nicer cars were not much more expensive than the cars I had been looking at. So, I began looking at cars that really make my heart sing, that had the stigma of only being purchased by the wealthy.

I test drove one, and as my hubby and I drove down the street, I felt all the things in that car. I felt excited and had goosebumps the whole ride. The thing I loved the most? I LOVED the ambient lighting—I could change the color to anything my little heart desired in the moment.

I took the steps to purchase the car and was planning on picking it up the next day. That evening, I lay in bed and worried relentlessly about what others might think of me. Would they think I was stuck-up? Would new clients think I was making too much money? Would I drive people away from me instead of toward me? Would I lose friends?

I asked God to provide the answers. Was I being selfish and would it be better to use this money for charity, or could I possibly be okay buying this car? My answer was, "Wendy, you can own anything you want and create everything and anything. The only person holding you back is you. You can buy the car . . . AND give to charity."

That was a humbling moment. My almighty God wanted to bless me, and I only needed to learn to receive.

We learn to receive when we are no longer attached to the thought that, if we need help, we are not enough. We learn to receive when we recognize that the collective is so much more powerful than the individual and that we alone can only do so much. We learn to receive when we do shadow work and discover the hidden traumas that are holding us back. We learn to receive when we stop self-betraying and say what we mean and mean what we say.

Most women I know struggle with receiving. There is something tied to their self-worth if they choose to receive help or money. The world has told them that women are to serve and give and nurture. And strong women never receive help.

Bullshit. I call bullshit on that one.

Women that don't learn how to find that beautiful balance in giving *and* receiving are on a sure road to burnout and resentment. And ladies, you aren't showing up in your highest and best if you are tired and pissed off at the world.

Receive.

Breathe that in for a moment. How would it feel to actually know that you are worthy of everything you seek? How would it feel to have many hands to make light work? How would it feel to receive the very things you have been worrying about?

What if you knew that you were the very dam that was blocking everything from you?

It's true. And if you are the very reason you aren't receiving, then you have the ability to teach and program yourself with a new way of thinking and being and showing up in this world. One that honors you and allows you to become the greatest version of yourself. One that will allow you to find more joy and peace than you ever thought was possible.

It's within you, not without.

What a liberating and amazing feeling it is when we know we can actually do something about the pain we are experiencing.

I am certain that many of you are wondering where to begin. I have some ideas that may work for you, to help you start the process of loving yourself and remembering who you are at the core. Then you can step into a higher vibration and learn to receive.

Your birthright entitles you to all the abundance in the world, my friend.

Points to Ponder:

- Raise your vibration each day. If things are feeling a bit heavy, break up the pattern by doing something you love. Dance around the house, get the paints out, write in your journal, talk to a friend that makes you laugh, take a yoga class. The choice is yours—simply do something each day to help you raise that frequency.

- Stop worrying about it. The more you dwell on your financial problems, the greater the problem becomes. Where our focus goes, energy flows. Focus on what you want, not on what you don't. We often feel like the only way to figure things out is to fixate on solutions. It actually drives the answers away from us. Focus on something else and raise that vibration and the answers will come to you.

- Write down your money story. Do you remember what your parents' money story was? Did money bring pain or happiness to your family? What stories did you create? Write them down, look at them, and then burn the paper you wrote those stories down on.

Chapter 13

TRUTH ABOUT SEX

I could hear the beat of the drum. More accurately, I could hear the beat of many drums—twenty-one in total. I had been magnetized toward this place and time for a while. It was as if my spirit knew that I needed to be in this place for me to progress and draw closer to myself and to God.

This drum retreat was in May of 2021. Just five months earlier, New Years' Eve, I had decided to sit in a beautiful bubble bath instead of participating in the regular antics I usually enjoyed. As I lay in the tub, I asked God what word I would choose for the year. What intention would I have? In a normal year, I would have written a two-page list of goals and committed myself to better health, more wealth, and new cars and homes.

But not this year. I had loved the time during Covid when I didn't need to do anything, be anywhere, or be on high alert every day. I wanted more of THAT.

I felt a bit guilty inside that I didn't desire to do more. I had learned to "do" my whole life and had equated "doing" to progressing forward. If I wasn't "doing," then I was regressing.

But then a familiar feeling washed over me, and I knew it was from Source and not from my mind.

"What if you were to simply BE this year?"

Oh, that sounded delicious. Was that even a thing? Could I potentially live life and not try so hard to improve and become "more," and simply be okay with where I was in that moment?

I didn't know, but I certainly wanted to take the chance and try it out. I knew from experience that each time I trusted that peaceful and glorious feeling, I would always be led on a journey of true discovery.

The thought of *being* meant to simply listen and be directed to what would come next. It wasn't a preplanned list of items, but a gentle tugging on my soul to notice things that would be valuable in learning to simply *be*.

This retreat was one of them. I had never actually paid for a retreat before. I was usually asked to speak or participate in the production of the retreat in some manner. Because I had experienced several retreats in this way, I didn't usually sign up for retreats as a consumer of them.

But this time it was different. The coordinator of the retreat was this fiery redhead who drew me in. I had watched from the sidelines as she posted different things on social media. We had become friends through other friends, yet we had never met. As I looked at her images and read her words, it was as if I KNEW her.

Hollie Hope. I even loved her name.

In early January, I kept noticing the event she was creating for May. We would make drums and play them, eat healthy food, and be around other amazing women.

Hmm....make drums? Play drums? Why was this calling to me?

I didn't know, but I was drawn like a moth to a flame.

I finally went online to sign up for the retreat, and when I clicked the "register" button, my spirit leapt up and down. I knew that this experience would be life-changing and the relationships I would form would be timeless.

That May, I was at this retreat, banging on these drums made from elk, deer, buffalo, and horse hides, and feeling things I had never felt before. Hollie had mentioned to me that as we started this process, we would stir up emotions that had been trapped, and that was part of the magic of the drum.

The very first sound we ever hear is our mother's heartbeat. We bond with the sound of beating and the gentle inhalation and exhalation of the breath. It is soothing and captivating and resonates with all of us on a deep level—a feeling of finally coming home.

It was the second day, and we had experienced two drum circles already. As I started to shift and notice my body, I realized that "it" was coming up again.

SHIT!

Seriously, I had worked for four years on healing my sexual traumas. I had utilized EMDR, hypnotherapy, energy work, acupuncture, Ortho-bionomy, nutritional guidance, and endless hours of prayer and meditation—I thought I was done with this chapter.

I was seriously tired of this endless loop of healing my sexuality. I was sick of it and I wanted to work on something else, anything else.

But here it was—the feeling, the fear, the anxiety, the grief, the loss, the powerlessness. It was all here now for me to view and decide what to do next.

I was invited to stand in the middle of the circle with other people, and the women started to drum around us. Up and down, various beats, beautiful singing, gently shaking up my cells so that the residual energy of those violations would finally be released. Up and down, vibration after vibration, beat after beat, I could feel it rising to the surface.

The next part simply cannot be put into words. There are no words to convey the power of a circle of women encircling me with their arms, guiding me through the release that would set me free. That grounded, fiery redhead helped me finally be unchained from the thing that held me back for far too long. I was wrapped in twenty arms, surrounded by all the others, and cradled by an angel who gently sang into my ear.

And . . . I was finally untethered, free of the shame, guilt, resentment, anger, grief, and suffering that had held me hostage for four decades.

I returned home from that retreat a different woman than the one I had been before. I realized that this release had given me the opportunity to start a brand new chapter in my life, though I wouldn't know how profound the changes would be for another month.

Two weeks after the retreat, I woke up in the middle of the night.

"What the hell just happened?" I asked myself.

I had experienced a pulse of energy in my sensual center that I had never experienced before.

I realized I had never before experienced anything even close to that wonderful feeling. I had always enjoyed sex, but honestly felt that, while it could be kind of fun for women, it was really meant for the man's pleasure. I certainly didn't understand why people wrote songs about it.

As I tuned in to what I had just experienced, I felt this need to learn more about my body. I don't believe I had ever even looked at my body before. I was raised in a culture where we didn't dress in front of others anywhere, not even in front of other women in the gym locker-room.

I had been introduced to the book, *Come As You Are: The Surprising New Science That Will Transform Your Life*, in which the author invites the reader to take a look in the mirror at the magnificent parts of our anatomy that are tucked away from view most of the time.

I looked with curiosity at every area in this "hidden" region that most of my life had been a source of pain and confusion rather than a place of refuge and peace and love.

That weekend my husband was going on a fishing trip with his friends and I decided to take myself on a date.

I dressed up in a beautiful outfit and lit candles around the room. I put on beautiful music and diffused my favorite essential oils into the room. I sat in a beautiful bubble bath and then got in the sauna. I was gentle, loving, kind, and patient. I decided to take my time and allow myself to actually "feel" this time, to learn how to receive pleasure and to have this experience be all about me.

And . . . it happened.

I had this surge of energy that ran through my body and down the core of my being. It pulsed and waved and danced through me as though I had unleashed a tidal wave of pleasure that had been stored away for decades.

And I cried.

I cried unceasing tears of joy, tears of gratitude that I had finally shed enough layers to fully receive pleasure and believe I was worthy to be loved in a way that I had never allowed before. I was alive. I was whole. I was resuscitated from a life of mediocrity and suffering and propelled into a place of absolute connection to the Divine.

I cried tears of sadness that I had never let myself experience this before, that the pain of what had occurred in my past was the story that would haunt me my entire life.

And now I was free.

I have only shared this story with a handful of people but each time I do, I see the power of my story help others to unlock their own sexuality and realize that we have been lied to all of our lives.

By now, the video of this story has most likely been received by many in the world. I never meant to share this very private place in my heart, but after seeing the change and hope and healing in those who could relate, I couldn't be selfish and keep it to myself.

The world would have us think that sex is equal to sin, that our sexuality is to be kept under wraps and that if we have the natural desire to feel and explore it, we are somehow dirty and something is wrong with us at the core.

Those of us who experienced abuse early in our lives often experience sex as a trigger of pain and suffering, and many times engage in sex out of a sense of duty to our partner, rather than as a way to connect, in the most sacred and divine way, with each other and with the source of creation.

The crown chakra was originally called the bliss chakra. They called it this because when we have an orgasm, the crown chakra opens up and we are closer to the Divine than at any other time in our lives.

Does it make sense that there has been an incredible effort to keep sexual power away from women for millennia?

During the witch trials in Europe and America, beautiful and charismatic women who had a voice were demonized and burned at the stake for showing any sort of power.

Even priests were able to condemn a woman if she aroused him and rejected him.

Rather than celebrating the power of this sexual energy in women, there are people in every generation who have corrupted and twisted this power and punished women who are unafraid to harness and use it. Even with huge wins in women's rights, we still continue to hit a wall when it comes to sexual conversations.

I know, because up until a year ago, I couldn't even utter the word "masturbation." It would legitimately make me blush to even say that word, let alone discuss it.

And now that I am on the other side, I look back and wonder why. Why was it so challenging to have a conversation around sex? It is the one thing that almost every human will experience in their lifetime. We don't seem to have any problem talking about food, water, breathing, and even bowels, but heaven forbid we utter the S . . . E . . . X word!

Women of today have so many rights, and yet we still live in a sexually repressed society in which women are considered harlots and whores if they lean into pleasure.

Isn't it interesting that the very thing that made you and me is demonized and considered immoral? So, what does that mean about the core of who we are?

If sex is shameful, then does that mean we are somehow flawed, that we are born as sinful, filthy individuals?

How is this so? If we are born clean and unscathed, then how is sex bad? Isn't this connection one of the most beautiful gifts that God has given us?

I believe that the most holy things are also often the most attacked.

I believe that this is THE most sacred gift God gave to us.

The power of creation: to create life *and* to create pleasure. To become one, not only with a partner, but with Source Energy.

Through my own sexual liberation, I have discovered that God is found in pleasure and that alignment and creation are found in the blissful state of sexual union. This realization only came after my healing and my acceptance of who I am. After discovering the truth about sex, I have become closer to God than I ever have been.

I do not believe we can access our full powers as humans and souls without healing sexually.

Sexual pleasure is one of the best ways to manifest. In the moment of bliss, we are able to create with more power and intention than at any other time.

I have a friend who says that she is going to go have $50K sex (meaning she is manifesting $50,000 in money during sex), and sure enough, it doesn't take long before she receives it.

And men, I don't want to exclude you and your experiences. You aren't to blame for the sins of the past! So many men have also been victims of sexual abuse and have not been allowed to voice it. They suffer in silence and are told that "real men don't cry."

Please cry. For heaven's sake, cry and allow those emotions to escape and liberate you from the hell that has been created within your being.

We can choose to live in denial, like I did for four decades, and believe that our past sexual traumas are simply a part of our lives that we convince ourselves don't impacts anything. Or we can choose to heal and discover the power that comes to us when we heal that part of our lives.

I promise you that it is worth it. It has been the single most healing process I have gone through to date. Nothing has brought more insight, discovery, and alignment with Source than healing my sexual trauma.

Nothing.

I believe that when healing men and women come together and help others to heal, we will help to heal a broken and hurting world.

And women hold a special place in this healing process. Women foster change within their family units and give permission and inspiration for the men of the world to follow suit.

It is time to finally make peace and to honor this sacred space that has been neglected, loathed, and demonized. It is time to change our perception from disgust to reverence for the pure sanctity that this energy has always been.

Satnam. I am truth . . . You are truth . . . truth is our essence.

Let's get brave and heal together.

Points to Ponder:

- Recognize the ways sexual trauma has prevented you from being the most loving version of yourself. What ways do you show up to protect yourself? Do you have a wall that prevents others from getting close? Write these things down because seeing them on paper will help you to see how they have indeed impacted your life. Awareness is the beginning of healing: exposing the darkness to the light in order to heal.

- Find ways to feel pleasure each day. It can be anything and does not necessarily need to be sexual. Even washing dishes can be pleasurable when we take the time to truly experience the sensations involved with warm sudsy water and the satisfaction of cleaning. Allow yourself to feel pleasure. Write about your experiences and start to find pleasure in the mundane and the normal.

Chapter 14
TRUTH ABOUT TRAUMA

I was in the shower, and Cory was washing me off. Why was I in the shower? And why was Cory crying?

"Cory, don't cry," I mumbled. It was hard to make sense of what was happening because I'd had so much to drink that night. "Why are you crying?" I asked again.

But I didn't remember the answer because I was in and out of awareness. All I could remember was that I had finally been invited to my ultimate crush's home that evening for a big party. Oh, I had longed for this moment for so long and here I was! My friend Meredith and I drove over in her Volkswagen Bug and I was ready to enjoy every moment of this magic.

The party was raging by the time we arrived. There was beer aplenty and I got involved in every beer game imaginable right out of the gate. As I got more inebriated, Cory mentioned that we should go upstairs together.

Yes!!

I get to make out with the guy of my dreams! Pinch me please!

And it was amazing . . . for a while. That's when drunk Wendy spoke too boldly and told him that I loved him. He stopped and sat upright. "What did you say?" I told him again that I was in love with him. Not that my seventeen-year-old self knew what that meant. I just knew I thought about him A LOT and apparently, I thought that was love.

He abruptly left the room and I recall crying a little bit, and that was when the boys walked in. I didn't recall this part for years, but it slowly seeped into my consciousness again at the exact time that my spirit was strong enough to withstand the ugliness, the vileness, and the destruction of the spirit of such a loving, sweet, and innocent young girl.

There they were—four of them. I see flashes of jeans, t-shirts, laughter, encouragement to do something so destructive that I don't believe they knew that their minutes of physical pleasure and power would be transferred into the cellular makeup of my body. And I froze. My response was to simply lie there and scream in my mind at the top of my lungs, "This is not a movie! This is real!!" This disgusting act of lust. This unbelievable horror of four boys taking every ounce of power and using it for their own pleasure. This act that would walk alongside me for four decades before I would be able to tell the truth and set it free.

This story may be the longest one in this book because it infused itself into every decision I made for decades. I didn't know it then, but it would deter me from who I was, the core of who I was, for longer than any other story, and it would hold me hostage.

As these memories started to unfold into my consciousness again, I started to look at them as simply "something that happened to me." Every once in a great while, if we were on a topic that brought up the subject, I would casually mention to my husband the rapes I had endured.

Four years ago, my body had finally had enough. It had stored the pain and guilt and suffering that I had experienced for far too long, and it knew I was finally resilient enough to withstand what was to come.

But this would prove to be one of the most challenging experiences of my life. The breakthrough would only come after the absolute breakdown. My trapped memories, emotions, and buried trauma were starting to surface. And like the pain a baby chick must endure while breaking out of its shell, so I had to endure the pain of breaking free from mine.

And it wouldn't simply be emotional. Every storage facility in my body would start to open to allow the toxicity to escape from my body. And in my case, this would play out in every type of pain you can imagine: physical, emotional, mental, and spiritual.

The greatest physical pain that I experienced during that time was the fibromyalgia that started in my mid back and then radiated out to my shoulders, neck, and brain. It makes sense now that I understand a bit more about chakras—the pain started where my solar plexus is located. The solar plexus chakra is where we hold our power.

I realized that, in that moment that night, I had given all of my power to those boys. By lying there, totally frozen, I came to feel like I was absolutely powerless in my life. And from that experience I formed a deep belief that others controlled me, and that my body was meant for other people's pleasure and not my own.

One evening I was in so much agony that I called a friend to see if I could have one of her edibles. Even though this went against all of my current values, I was in absolute meltdown mode and after almost two years of not sleeping and being in constant, chronic pain, I didn't care. I simply did not care.

I took a very small amount and prayed that it would help me sleep. When that helped me calm down a little bit, I decided to take a bit more and went to bed feeling groggy for the first time in months.

An hour later, I noticed my brain spinning out of control. I felt utterly unable to stop the pictures flashing in my mind. I could not concentrate on anything for a singular moment, and all of the tools to calm my nervous system were going out the window. That out-of-body experience would prove to be one of the greatest meltdowns of my life.

I screamed, at the top of my lungs, at my husband . . .

"Get your fucking gun and shoot me!! Shoot me!! If you love me, you will fucking kill me! I cannot take it anymore! I can't do this anymore!"

Over and over I shouted this. My loving husband, cradling my head in his lap, made soothing statements, "Wendy, I love you, I would never hurt you. Breathe. Breathe and look at me. I am here. I am safe. I am near you. I will never let you go. Focus on me and breathe."

After taking two Xanax, I finally relaxed enough to sleep. The next day when I woke up, I found my husband sitting at the table.

"Wendy, what happened last night will NEVER happen again. I want to figure out what is at the root of this. Let's make a list of what you have done, what you haven't done, and what may be something we need to consider."

As we made the list, my husband got a look in his eye like he had made a connection.

"Wendy, you talk about getting raped like you had lunch with a friend. You don't show any emotion whatsoever, and yet you are the most emotional person I know. Something doesn't add up with that. What if the thing you haven't considered is that it is time to work on the trauma you experienced in those moments?"

I admitted that perhaps it was something I could work on. It occurred to me that I had signed up to go to Younique Foundation's retreat called The Haven Retreat. I had never attended a retreat at that point and my nonprofit was considering starting them as a part of the You Got This network. I had selfishly signed up because I had heard that it was free to those who had been sexually violated before the age of eighteen and knew I met the criteria. They had been emailing me dates to attend for the previous three months.

And as God would have it, they had a last-minute opening and I signed up for the next retreat available, which was a week away.

I drove to the retreat and arrived at the home that would allow me some of the greatest healing of my life. I recall watching the gates to the estate open up and feeling like God had brought me to heaven in order to facilitate my healing. I was placed with seven other women who would become the angels that would stand next to me as I felt the pain. They are still in my life to this day. This was the beginning of my healing and freeing myself for good.

While this story is specific to sexual abuse, I believe every human on the earth at this time has experienced trauma.

Think about your own life. Have you experienced a loss such as a death, miscarriage, or divorce? Have you experienced financial ruin and filed bankruptcy, or a period of homelessness? Were you bullied in high school, or physically beaten by parents or loved ones?

I can't think of a person I know who hasn't experienced trauma. If trauma is a part of your story, then the memories and emotions are stored in your body. Period. This is the truth and with truth, you can either go into acceptance and learn to feel and move through the emotions, or you can continue trying to shut off emotions by taking pills, being a workaholic, eating food, or having sex.

You either numb, or you move into a place of utter acceptance and forgiveness.

You may even think to yourself, "I am doing well in my life. My past experiences are not trauma, and they are not impacting my life."

Maybe. You could be right. You could be one of the exceptions who didn't place any meaning on your experiences at all. You were able to filter those experiences through and not store any emotion at all after experiencing something monumental in your life.

Or, like many others, you have placed meaning on your past experiences and then tucked them away in a box in a very safe place in your heart. This box keeps you from truly connecting with others and from feeling full joy and love, and yet it protects you, doesn't it? There is justification that since these emotions are so intense, it is better to feel nothing, or to feel anything other than THIS.

But is it really?

Do you really want to experience life as a zombie? Or worse, as someone who reacts to everything because your system can't handle "one more thing"? Maybe you are a hothead and people have to tiptoe around you because they don't know if you are going to be the nice version of yourself today or whether you will erupt in an overflowing lava of anger and frustration.

So, let's get real. Trauma impacts you. It impacts you big time, and doesn't allow you to have the life that you deserve, the life you yearn for. It is what is standing between you and your hopes and dreams.

Bessel van der Kolk, in her book, *The Body Keeps the Score: Brain, Mind, and Body in the Healing of Trauma*, writes, "Once you start approaching your body with curiosity instead of fear, everything shifts."

It takes bravery to actually hold something up and look at it, rather than stuff it under the rug and balance furniture over it, as we often do. Only by confronting our demons can we heal them. And for many of us, this feels paralyzing. We can't imagine re-examining something that we experienced or something we did to others. But under the right guidance, we can start the process and release the binds that hold us hostage, and literally set ourselves free of the emotional and spiritual pain that it placed upon us.

The other option we can choose is to have our bodies beg for us to listen. As we numb with one thing or another, the body gets clever and finds another way to remind us that our trauma is still there, ready to be healed. The body will remind you that you are so much stronger than you give yourself credit for, and that if you choose to come to terms with trauma, your healing will allow you to remember who you are behind the façade of the external world.

I believe that this is the most courageous thing we will ever do as humans: feeling the things that we can't believe or don't want to believe actually happened to us.

The beautiful thing is that there are so many inspired modalities that can help us now.

We simply need to choose one that resonates with us at this time. I started with a therapeutic technique called EMDR, which is short for Eye Movement Desensitization and Reprocessing. In this technique, a therapist guides eye movement and tones, or taps, to move a memory that has been incorrectly stored. A good analogy is an open cut that keeps being exposed to elements that keep it from healing. Once it is protected and cared for, the body can heal the cut easily and without additional stress on the body. Our mental state is similar. Once a trauma happens, it is processed and stored, unprotected and vulnerable. Any event that triggers this occurrence will cause the trauma to react. EMDR helps to protect and care for it so it can then heal on its own.

There are other techniques that can do the same thing and may work better for you. I suggest trying to find the technique that resonates most with you. You may end up utilizing many of them in your healing journey.

Here are a few ideas: AIT, hypnotherapy, Ortho-bionomy, energy work, Reiki, massage, tapping, and plant medicine.

All techniques have the same goal: to help move the stuck emotional energy and the memory associated with it, and release and store it in a different manner.

There are several things you can do without any training at all. EFT (emotional freedom technique), or tapping, is one of those techniques. It is similar to acupressure and focuses on tapping points that stimulate the central nervous system and release helpful chemicals. I have successfully utilized this technique to help move intense emotions and rewrite subconscious stories from past trauma. This one is free and everyone has access to the instruments: your fingertip and your voice.

Many forms of healing are even approved to be billed through medical insurance. I love it when science catches up with miracles! I have seen things work for years before research substantiates what my heart has always known. Energy work will be one of those one day. I truly believe in my heart that research will show that certain techniques help shift energy and allow it to be released by the body.

And that release is where the healing starts. When the emotional response is changed, we find a way to release the trapped emotions. And then we can learn how to release other emotions that filter into our lives as they come, instead of playing clean up later, when those emotions have had an opportunity to morph into something much greater and larger than they were before.

Regardless of the modalities that you end up using, just start with something.

These traumas are keeping you from being your highest and best.

It is challenging to see the light of the soul when it is surrounded by the darkness of despair through traumatic events. As layers fall off, you will start to feel lighter and more peaceful.

It is a process, and the great news is that some of these modalities work quickly and efficiently. The biggest commitment needed is that you show up and do the work, that you choose something and stick with it for a while until you start to see the subtle shifts happening.

You may start to see the beauty in things around you in greater detail. You may find yourself laughing again. Maybe you'll find yourself dancing around your home when a great song is playing. Regardless of your response, you are worth healing, my friend. You cannot bring your special light to this world if it is dimmed by the weight of your experiences.

It is time to set yourself free.

Points to Ponder:

- Learn how to tap. Nick Ortner with The Tapping Solution has an incredible channel on YouTube. You can learn the basics of the technique and also be guided by specific emotions you are dealing with.

- At the very least, watch how trauma interferes with your life. Do you avoid certain situations? Do you feel anxiety, even when you can't find a valid reason to feel it? Do you wish you could be closer in your relationships but have this inner knowing that you won't let people in, and that you have built a wall to protect yourself? Write down your feelings in a journal as you unpack the impact that trauma has played in your life.

- Pay special attention to Chapter 19: The Truth about Judgment. The more intense the trauma, usually the more intense the internal judgment was created in that moment.

Chapter 15

TRUTH ABOUT PLANT MEDICINE

For about a year, I had been called to look into plant medicine. I looked into it very carefully and with much caution, knowing that the medicine would only be as powerful as the facilitator curating the experience.

My intention was to break the chains of depression that seemed to find its grip on most of my family members: my father, my grandmother, my children, and myself. Two had already died from the coping mechanisms that they chose to use, and I was ready to fight the fierce battle to break the chains that bound our family.

I knew in my heart that I didn't need to "accept" that this was simply a part of our genetic makeup. It was time to show that we could collectively heal and that if I chose to go within and battle those demons, we would all win.

I found someone who would hold a sacred space and love me through the journey.

When I arrived, I looked around the room at six beautiful women, all feeling nervous and yet having the inner knowing that the earth held power to help us heal.

I found my small mat in a rose-petal adorned safe space that would hold me for the next eight hours. As I sipped the tea that would provide the power of change, I was nervous, but I reminded myself to trust myself completely. My heart had brought me here to heal its wounds and strip away the heart wall I had created to save my life. This heart wall had served its purpose, but I knew where I was going and that wall needed to come down. The power of love was in that beautiful space, and with its freedom came peace, love, and service to others.

My future was one of love. My future was one of serving and providing words to a hurting world—words of truth that would resonate within their souls, knowing that it was time to collectively heal together.

As I felt the medicine course through my body, I lay down and immediately felt a surge of energy. The energy was so incredibly strong that it scared me. It was like starting the birthing process and wondering if you could actually do it as you felt the transition set in during labor.

There is no going back, only within, and it was time to fight my demons.

As I was feeling it, I kept asking when it would end. The loving internal guide and golden teacher that accompanied me on my journey—the one I could hear but couldn't see—whispered, "Where is this end you keep asking about? There is only now."

"When is the pain going to go away? I want an end; I need to know there is an end."

The teacher said, "It is time to surrender to now . . . now is all you have."

As I learned to surrender on that tiny mat, I felt my body vibrate to such a high capacity that I didn't know if my body could withstand the intensity of it.

I felt this amazing feeling sweep over my body, and was told, "This is what love feels like. Real love. You have felt a tiny glimpse of what love is, but this is pure love."

In that space, I felt pure love—no guilt, no shame—and the realization that I was the only one holding myself hostage in the pain I was feeling.

After a few hours of feeling this blissful state, it was time to do what I had come for:

Release.

Release the toxic thoughts, behaviors, and stories. And it started with purging the emotions.

There are no words for what happened next. The intense flow of emotions that seeped from my body was overwhelming. Sobs wracked my body and shook it for hours: eight hours, to be precise.

And I felt them all: the sorrow, the grief, the regret, the guilt, the shame, the judgment, and the utter hopelessness that I placed in every area of my life.

I understood what it meant to "feel in order to heal."

At times I didn't think I would withstand the pain. The fear and the darkness and the sorrow felt like it would swallow me whole.

But . . . I did it.

I effing did it.

It was without a doubt the hardest thing I had ever done up until that point in my life.

Yep—harder than childbirth.

But the following day, I felt a fog lift off of my body and mind that I had never experienced before.

This . . . this is what peace feels like.

This is what joy feels like.

This is what it feels like to feel light.

I could see nature in greater depth and with all of the colors popping out in full force.

How did I not see this before?

I listened to music as I walked my dog, and I "felt" the music. I started to dance down the street, laughing and giggling at the lightness of life.

"Why did I take things so seriously before?" I thought.

One of the greatest blessings of taking that plant journey was that I caught a glimpse of the creative power we have in this life. My life is literally outlined by myself and God. We co-create it together. The two of us designed every single experience for my highest and best good.

This understanding made me feel lighter, walk a little taller, and realize that I cannot get this life wrong. I legitimately couldn't mess it up.

The weight lifted off of my shoulders.

As I returned home, I sat at my sacred writing space and looked over at photos of Christ, and remembered my grandmother and my father.

I had been told for years that my grandmother was always with me. I had felt impressed to dig a little deeper into knowing her, since she died before I was born.

She lived a life of suffering. She spent the last twenty years of her life intoxicated and numbing out life. It was simply too much for her. As a result, she didn't get to see her children grow up and mature and become amazing humans.

My father, her son, followed suit. Although he was an insanely successful businessman, he held deep demons that finally consumed him in a similar pattern.

One too many rehabs.

One too many pills.

He too would die before his time.

Oh, how I miss him. I miss his voice, his charisma, his larger-than-life presence.

But he was here with me in this moment.

They both were.

They were cheering and celebrating that I hadn't simply felt the emotions for myself, but I had broken the chains that had bound them too.

We were free; the price had been paid, the emotions felt, the pain released.

I looked at my painting of Christ, the one I love because the artist had based it on the Dead Sea Scrolls writings. It is not the usual Caucasian-based drawing, but one of His actual face, with His tender eyes staring lovingly back at me.

Yes, He had shown me how. In the Garden of Gethsemane, He felt all of it. He experienced every emotion to the point that his body bled from every pore.

He is the perfect example of what we can become. Maybe He is the Savior because He is showing us how to walk His path and save ourselves so that we can be "at one" again with Him and God and Mother and learn what it is to become enlightened.

Maybe it's more than simply believing—maybe it's feeling.

Maybe . . .

I don't have to have it all figured out, but I do believe that when we feel the emotion that we have trapped inside of ourselves, we will be free.

Emotions are simply "energy in motion." When emotions are stagnant, they can become residue to our souls, blocking us from remembering who we are, from feeling the peace and love that flow freely through us, and that takes away our joy.

It is interesting that right after I had this experience, Netflix released *How to Change Your Mind*, which is an exploration into psychedelics and the power that they have to heal the mind and the body.

In this series, individuals share stories of releasing PTSD, OCD, depression, and anxiety, and the power of plant medicine in that release. The hope is that something here can have a profound positive impact on our lives.

Mother Earth has indeed given us everything we need in order to heal.

It is said that many psychedelics were banned in the 60s and 70s because individuals were waking up to who they were. Those in power and control and government did not like having an "awakened" population. A population of people that know this secret would no longer be controllable.

The beautiful thing today is that information is almost instantaneous now. It is next to impossible to stop every bit of information from passing on in a viral way, especially information that could set an entire species free from restraint and suffering.

Even research is catching up. The research on ketamine is astounding, showing that suicide ideation is turned off almost immediately after only one session. Some doctors are even using breathwork in combination with administering ketamine or psilocybin to assist the healing process.

The power of plants is to be respected and used intentionally. Frivolous usage for fun will not heal; it will simply be used as another way to numb, distract, and avoid, which is what most of us have done our whole lives.

One of the issues in the 60s was that plant medicine was used without restraint or respect. It was used in excess to avoid life. The key to the benefits of using plant medicine is that we focus our intention on respect, love for ourselves, and our connection to all things.

Deliberate usage of plants for healing will give us another tool to set us free.

Free to remember who we are.

Free to remember how powerful we are.

Free to open up our heart space and allow love to flow in and to flow out.

It took me a long time to embrace plants. I was taught from an early age that these substances were evil and not of God. It took watching one of my sons take his mental health into his own hands and demand that the only thing that was setting him free was the use of THC. He moved to a state that legalized marijuana usage and I saw the transformation in my child. Where pharmaceuticals were giving him suicidal thoughts and making things worse, plant medicine helped him to calm his busy brain and allowed him to flow through life in ease.

I don't believe that Satan or evil would have anything to do with this beautiful healing change in my son. I believe it was his heart that led him to that choice and I love and respect plants for the power of healing they can provide when used respectfully.

There are many plants and resources to explore and consider. Your heart will tell you if any are useful for your healing and will also let you know if they are not.

The plants explored in the four-part documentary *How to Change Your Mind* are LSD, psilocybin, peyote, and MDMA.

In addition to the four explored in the documentary, there is ketamine, which is FDA approved for use with doctor assistance.

Most of these plant medicines are still illegal, though a few are legal with religious exemptions. Drugs such as MDMA are still illegal except in clinical trials.

There are a few states that are opening up to legalizing mushrooms, so simply be aware of which states are allowing what. You do want to follow the laws of your land, but know you can travel if necessary to get the treatment you need.

My strongest advice is to find someone that is curating a beautiful healing experience. Find out how many journeys they have facilitated, what their background is, and how they will be facilitating. Are they also still on their own journey, or will they be fully available to assist you in your transition and healing?

I highly encourage you to find someone who will be available to you emotionally, physically, and spiritually if you choose to go down this road. Your facilitator will allow you to feel and will not interfere, and will secure a safe environment full of love and heart opening space to embrace your emotions and set them free.

There are many other modalities that can and will work for you to heal. Many of them will take many sessions and possibly years of work, and that is okay for many of us.

However . . . I wanted to get shit done. That is kind of my personality. I have had opportunities to work with individuals that are very intuitive and they all say that even my spirit is a "get er' dun" kind of gal.

I am kind of crazy in love with her. She is pretty amazing and brave and courageous.

And I laugh at her often because she has a special flavor of crazy.

Because of this trait, I wanted an experience that would allow me to release as much as I could physically handle in a 24-hour period. And while that was the most challenging thing I have done to date, it created a way for me to show up differently almost immediately. It helped rewire neural pathways that were damaged from the stressful lifestyle I had chosen for so many years, and it changed my perspective immediately.

Since then, I have experienced small "micro doses" of plant medicine. I choose to only utilize them when my heart directs me to that experience and then partake of the minimum amount that is sufficient for me. During these experiences I have learned profound insights into myself, the world I have created, and the true connection that exists between all things.

I have had moments where I see a pelican land gracefully into the water and cry tears of joy for the miraculous beauty I have just beheld. I have had opportunities to look at trees and bushes and see their radiant vitality and pure joy they have in simply existing. They teach me, they connect with me, and they help me to feel more connection to myself and to others.

I have a deep reverence for Mother Earth and all she has for us. There are lessons to learn by simply observing and watching how nature interacts and exists in this world. They are never in a hurry, they are surrendering to different weather conditions and patterns, and they ebb with the seasons, allowing the natural flow of life to go through them.

Wouldn't it be amazing if we were able to imitate this in our own lives?

If your heart is leading you here, ask for help and assistance from the other side to ensure you are being led to the right place and the right medicine.

It is here for your healing and your awakening.

It is time to Illuminate your Essence, my friend.

The time is now.

Points to Ponder:

- Watch the Netflix docuseries *How to Change Your Mind.*
- There are so many resources online about the benefits of plant medicine now. Do your research, trust your heart, and ask to be led to the websites that will be most beneficial for your learning and understanding as you consider this modality in your healing journey

Chapter 16

TRUTH ABOUT THE PRESENT

I could hear the crunch under my feet as I walked out onto the Paradise Rim Trail. The intense red mountains call to my soul each and every day. The contrast of the blue skies and white billowy clouds outline each jagged peak perfectly.

I could smell the dirt and the intoxicating aroma of the trees in bloom at the end of springtime. A beautiful yellow and black butterfly was soaring right in front of me, reminding me that I am always evolving and shedding layers of old in order to become what has always been.

I put my AirPods in and listened to piano ballads. My heart soared with the sounds and notes that were playing. I could feel every cell in my body respond: I am awake, I am alive.

I was there with no other agenda but to simply be—be present with the world in this moment—and I recognize the greatness of that intention. I walked along with the full consciousness and love that exists in the Universe when I choose to step out of my stories, my endless loop of thoughts, and my daily agenda that will never run out of items to be checked off.

Only two months prior had I made the conscious shift of choosing to share my gifts with the world: my gifts of expression and communication, which I had stuffed away because of the pain they had caused me in the past. Realizing those were stories that could be re-written, I was living a completely different life. I was no longer racing from appointment to appointment in search of the next "fix" of financial resources that would be traded for my inner peace.

And here I was, seeing life in a different way. I looked around and felt the love that radiated through the rocks, the trees, the wind, the clouds, the sky, and realized it was all an extension of me. I never saw it before because I was always running to things outside of me that promised me the feeling of accomplishment and success.

Where had I been running to? I had heard this voice several times. The voice kept saying, "There is no other place to run but here, right now, at this moment. Stop chasing your imagination and start living."

As I walked, I felt connected to that voice in a way that I couldn't be before.

The book I was writing had morphed into several projects as I opened my heart and was receptive to receiving whatever came my way. These projects didn't translate into business like my former career—they were simply joyful to receive with the opportunity to co-create.

I started to see in my mind visions of the video I would be filming in a month. I had this urge to consider a video and now it was unfolding in all of its detail right in front of me: every scene, the tender display of emotion, and the scenes that will help draw individuals into the story I have lived and breathed.

And it is glorious.

Creation will only unfold in the present moment.

The perfect alignment of Divine Source can only be received by the Holy Instant—this moment and this time.

Our ego would say we need to chase the Holy Instant to catch it somehow in flight. But we will simply get exhausted and overwhelmed and frustrated, because the Holy Instant only occurs when we can get quiet and so we can "be" with it in the now.

It has often been called the Holy Present of Presence.

To be present is to be alive, to feel all of our human senses in order to receive our divine senses.

The checklist of life will never get us to this end destination. Living in the future will never help us to stop being worried, and playing our past on autopilot will never change the outcome of what has happened.

The Perfect Present.

The Holy Now.

The Spirit.

The Power of Now.

You will receive and become the peaceful and blissful being that you are when you stop trying and start being.

Becoming like a little child means living right now, in the present moment.

Can you imagine a life with no care, no worries, and no anxiety? The present moment holds that promise, if we will just consider staying in its glorious majesty. *A Course in Miracles* says, "There is no hell. Hell is only what the ego has made of the present, because you are afraid of it. Fear is not of the present, but only of the past and future, which do not exist." It is called the present moment, the Holy Instant, and in this place everything makes sense, everything feels peaceful and calm. In this moment, clarity is received and doubts are washed away. Most of us live very little of our time in the present. Our mind wanders to our to-do list or focuses on the mistakes of the past. When we do this, we miss the beauty in what is, and we create our own living and breathing hell right here on Earth.

So how do we begin to rewire this programming?

You start with this present moment right now. Tap into your sensations. What do your five senses tell you? Feel aroused in those feelings. Arousal is not necessarily sexual nor necessarily felt in our sexual center. It is felt throughout the body, igniting the senses and the mind. Arousal in its simplest form means "waking up." We are asleep much of the time. This process wakes you up and helps you to remember who you are. Many of us have been completely shut off to our bodies, so we don't recall what this feels like. So simply tuning in and enjoying those sensations is a foreign concept at first. But it gets easier the more you practice.

Tune in right now. Close your eyes and breathe in for four, hold for four, breathe out for four, hold for four. Do this four times. Now just simply be the observer.

- What do you feel?
- Does your skin give you any type of sensation?
- Are you hot or cold?
- What are you seeing?
- Are you inside or outside?
- What colors do you see?
- Do you see movement?
- What do you smell?
- Do you taste anything?
- What do you hear?
- Does anything evoke emotion?

It's amazing how this quick exercise, practiced regularly, can change your life. Right now, I am sitting outside on a patio in a beautiful desert community. I feel the gentle breeze on my body. I see a beautiful lake in the distance that is a vibrant blue and palm trees with green and brown. I see the shadows of quail walking along the porch. I am listening to meditation music, which has a calming effect on me. I taste coffee on my tongue, and smell flowers from the bushes next to me. I feel my skin tingling with the cool breeze, and emotions of gratitude, love, and peace come to me.

While I am doing this, I sense my mind wanting me to address the daily items of business. I simply see those items and choose to focus on other things. What I have found is that the more I do this, the less I find it frustrating that my ego continues to want to sabotage this moment. It is there, I know it is there, and I simply choose to be in the present moment.

It's a choice. And when we are in the Holy Instant, we will start to recognize our truth and create a heaven instead of hell while we are here in this existence.

Our ego will fight against this statement. I mean, why on earth would you consider creating hell if you didn't have to? Isn't that a situation that God put into your life so you could learn through challenges and life lessons?

Perhaps. However, nowhere in our lesson are we required to think self-deprecating thoughts, use self-betrayal or judgment, and beat ourselves up incessantly. It is suffering that isn't required for the lesson. And yet, our natural self tends to wander down that path every time we get presented with something that is hard and challenging to navigate. We might have even put ourselves into that situation with the choices that we made. That's when the war inside gets really ugly. "It's my fault." "I always do this." "Why can't I get it right?" "I am an idiot." "No wonder no one loves me and can't stand me."

When we live in the Holy Instant, we don't live in the past. We don't continually rethink what we could have or should have done in those moments. They simply were. You experienced them, you survived them, and you get to experience something else now. If you've experienced a deep trauma, such as death, divorce, rape, or chronic illness, we will dive deep into healing trauma in another chapter. At this time, I would invite you to consider that you can release the trauma held deep within your body and once again be free.

Even in those moments, you can choose to step into the Holy Instant.

Not long ago, I experienced one of the worst stomach flus of my life. My stomach churned with cramps for several days, leaving me no energy for anything but staying in bed. The first day was horrific and I felt sorry for myself that I was suffering through this incredibly intense pain. The second day I woke up and a thought came into my mind. What if I could find joy in this moment right now? Is that possible? In the midst of stomach cramps, and rushing to the bathroom every hour, could I find joy?

As soon as I asked myself to open up to possibility, I remembered a 13-part series from Joe Dispenza that was on one of my favorite channels and decided that if I was going to be in bed, I would actually have time to watch this program that I felt impressed would bring wisdom and knowledge to me.

That day, as I watched each program, I felt a swelling of love and peace wash over me. I was choosing to step into accepting my situation and realizing that my choice on that day was to learn and experience a different perception in a difficult situation. The day went quickly and easily and I found myself relaxing into my body. My body started healing quickly and doing what it does best, which is to repair and come back into homeostasis.

What a profound lesson I discovered.

Each and every experience, lesson, and event can be an opportunity to choose to feel bliss and joy, or suffering and pain. It is here that we find true solace and comfort through the Holy instant.

In this instant you will discover the answers to your questions. The Holy Spirit won't be able to get through the web of to-dos and the constant barrage of thoughts that pervade your mind every minute of every day. The Holy Instant only happens when you are intentional with being here, right now, and quiet the mind so that the soul can speak.

The magic lies here, in this moment.

Each of us has two permanent guests in our reality here on Planet Earth. One is our ego, who will continually distract, numb, and lead us away from truth. The other is the spirit, or our soul, who will continually fill us with love, light, and knowledge as we start to forgive the world we have created.

When we start to wake up to the two distinct energies that exist within us, we will start to feel empowered to do something about it. The familiar way to describe the ego is the monkey mind. It is all over the place. It will fill us with fear, and talk us out of anything that will lead us to the discovery of what it really is. Its job is to keep us safe, but safety to the ego is familiar. That is why women in domestic violent relationships will stay. Their hearts will encourage them to honor themselves, but their egos will often scream much louder that it is safer to stay than to go.

From the outside this is madness. But how often do we stay stuck in life because it is familiar? How many of us stay in jobs that are slowly killing us, but we choose to stay because of the comfort of a paycheck rather than taking a risk for our soul?

And this is the part of us that will continually create chaos. When we feel out of sorts, it is usually because our heart is telling us one thing and our head is telling us another. The dichotomy of the two is what creates resistance.

Become an observer and look at what your mind is saying. It is honestly quite funny when you start to hear the dialogue. It is like some neurotic, panic-stricken entity that has taken up residence in our minds. Once you listen, you can start to recognize some truth to it.

You will start to see a pattern emerge when you pay attention. The ego will generally be encouraging you to bring up the past, or have you worrying about the future. The ego will bring up words like, could have, should have, and what if. Along with these thoughts you will notice the emotions that accompany them. When you are in the past you will generally feel regret and depression, while the future will bring anxiety and stress. These emotions are trying to gain your attention so that you will notice them and come back to the present.

The heart wants you to stay in the now. While your mind wanders and fills you with fear, the world awaits your presence so you can see the beauty in the now.

Where are we going anyways? Where are we always running to? Is there always something better out there in the future?

I was taught from a young age to "endure to the end." That we had to trudge through this lifetime so that we could have eternal bliss in the next.

Why? When it is possible to forgive this world right now and change our perspective so that we see a world free of pain and misery in the present.

It is time to create a new world for ourselves. A world full of beauty and grace. A world that exists right now, not in the next realm or the promise of something better after this lifetime. We have the opportunity to experience it right now.

Learning to be present, aware, grateful, and alive will change your life.

The truth is in the present.

Points to Ponder:

- Find an activity that helps you stay present. For me, yoga and hiking help me to focus on what is right in front of me and help me unify myself in that spirit-mind-body connection that is so important. I encourage you to find time for this activity at least once a week to start, and more often as you learn to love this state of life.

- Learn to recognize that space when you have inner chaos. You are usually in direct conflict between your heart and mind. Observe what is happening in your mind and choose what dialogue you are willing to have. Most of the time, your ego is pulling you into the future or the past. Help it come back to the present. That is where your power is, my friend.

- Write in your journal. Focus on gratitude and what you love. Look around you in the present moment and see the miracles that are staring you right in the face.

Chapter 17

TRUTH ABOUT SURRENDER

I was dying.

My body felt weak, frail, and tired.

Each day I would wake up to discover that I had lost more weight. My muscle was disappearing and some days I could only muster up enough strength to make it to my mailbox.

And because I am a doer, I had spent the last several years desperately trying to find the answers. I knew in my heart that there was an answer out there, and my only response was to search and throw spaghetti at the wall until something might stick.

After going to every doctor, specialist, coach, therapist, and functional medicine doctor, I had come up empty handed. I had purchased thousands of dollars in supplements in my closet in pursuit of the pill that would make it all go away.

I could see the hopelessness in my eyes as I looked in the mirror. I was beat down, beat up, and had no fight left in me.

On this night, I decided to surrender. I would give up and give it to God. I neither had the energy nor the desire to fight it anymore.

I asked my husband to kneel down and pray with me. As I spoke out loud to God, I heard myself say "My dearest Heavenly Father, I am submitting to your will. I know in my heart that I am dying and that I don't have much time left. If it is time to come home, I will surrender and willingly step through the veil. I want to thank you for the amazing ride I have had. I want you to know that I see the beauty and greatness in my life. I see visions of my life unfold before me and it has been magnificent. Thank you for my husband, my children, my parents and siblings. Thank you for the crazy adventures I have had and the miracles that I have witnessed while on this earth.

The only thing I ask for is to have a few more weeks or months to spend with my family. They are the only thing that matters to me at this moment.

But God, in my heart, I don't feel like it is my time. I feel like I am to do more, give more, and love more in my life. I feel like things are incomplete and that there is much more to experience while here on earth. If this is the case, please help me know what is inside of my body that is making me so sick. Is it a brain tumor? Is it cancer? The doctors can't seem to find it, and I know if I don't find it soon, I will soon be with you."

I had finally asked the right question in order to hear the right answer.

Within three days of this heartfelt plea to God, I had four friends say the exact same thing to me.

"Have you considered that your illness is related to your breast implants?"

These were individuals that never gave me their opinions and were friends that I respected and loved. When the fourth person asked the very same question, I looked up into the sky and said, "You are trying to tell me something, aren't you?"

I immediately started the research and discovered that there was a certain way in order to take my implants out properly, and that there needed to be a doctor very familiar with the process in order to help the body heal.

The next day, I immediately started calling each doctor on the approved breast implant illness list, and discovered that most everyone was booked for 6 months to one year.

I knew that I did not have that much time.

"God, please take me to the right doctor that can assist me in taking these breast implants out. You have given me the answer, now please help create a miracle so that I can get them out."

Within a few minutes I had a friend message me and tell me that she had just gotten her breast implants out, and that she used a doctor that was not on the list. She was a nurse and asked him all of the right questions and discovered that he was using the right techniques and modalities in order to ensure that the toxins would be extracted with the breast implants.

I called immediately. When the nurse answered, she reported that an opening for a consultation had just opened up that same day. I immediately drove the three hours to the doctor's office and as I explained my symptoms to the well-trained doctor, I saw his eyes fill with compassion as I reported my myriad of symptoms that had dozens of other doctors scratching their heads.

As I went through the list of brain fog, vertigo, insomnia, Hashimoto's, fibromyalgia, cystitis, UTI's, SIBO, leaky gut, chronic constipation, and severe anxiety and depression, he nodded his head in understanding.

"Wendy, you are reporting the same symptoms as many of the women who have breast implant illness, and I want you to know that you are not crazy. You are not making this up, and you are going to feel better very, very soon," he said.

Tears flowed. Tears from the years of pain. Tears from the constant belief that I was going crazy and that I was making this up. And tears for the confirmation that my body was indeed dying from forty toxic chemicals that had been leaching in my body for seven years.

As I sat in the room with the scheduling nurse, she again reported, "we happen to have an opening for a surgery next week, is that too soon?"

No, not too soon. In fact if it were any later it may have been too late.

Twelve days after discovering the truth, I was able to have an explant surgery performed and was given a new lease on life.

It was in the surrender that I received my answers.

It was the acceptance and stepping out of resistance that allowed me to be open to the truth.

I wouldn't be writing this book right now if I hadn't simply submitted to the Divine's will and learned to stop fighting and start trusting.

I consider myself a recovering control freak. I learned through my trauma and the stories that I created to stop trusting everyone, including God and myself.

The battle with breast implant illness was won when I surrendered. When I decided to let things go and let God, I became the victor.

How many times have we all tried to dot the i's and cross the t's in order to avoid conflict and failure? How many times have we stayed up at night trying to figure out the exact solution that will get us out of our plight?

And yet, most of the time we simply continue the cycle of frustration and suffering from that very worry and resistance.

When I turned my situation over to the Divine, I gave it to a trusted source that could see the whole picture. I didn't need to "figure things out," or run frantically around like a chicken with her head off anymore.

I had completely accepted my life with no changes. Either God would take me home, or I would find my answers. And I had resolved in my mind that either answer was okay.

In that surrender, I found peace and relaxed into life. And that is where the miracles unfold.

On one of my birthdays, my husband told me excitedly that he was "taking me on an adventure for a few days." He gave me a list of items to pack and on that list was the recommendation to bring "closed toe shoes." I thought that was really weird, but I packed accordingly and we set out on a five hour drive.

When we arrived, we checked into the hotel and then he took me to a river dinner cruise. As we watched the sunset from the deck on the boat, I felt an incredible closeness to this person who had really "scored" big time.

He then mentioned that I needed to wake up the next morning and wear my "closed-toe shoes."

The next morning he drove me to the small airport and I saw a sign that said, "scenic aerial tours." Again, I thought to myself, "wow, he is knocking this birthday adventure out of the park!"

Five minutes later, I was signing a waiver for a "skydiving adventure." I felt my breakfast coming up and was going on autopilot as I learned the basics of tandem jumping and the basic safety precautions.

Now you need to understand. I am terrified of heights. It is my greatest fear, and so far out of my comfort zone that it wasn't even in sight.

As luck would have it, they were behind schedule and so I got to spend over an hour in the hangar watching the instructors getting ready for their jumps. My heart felt like it would leap out of my chest.

At that moment, I decided I would have two options. I could either throat punch my husband for coercing me into this experience, or I could do something that I never thought I was capable of.

Lucky for my husband I chose the latter. I was being very gracious because he wasn't even going with me, he said he would be "cheering me on from the ground."

Yes, he is seriously demented sometimes.

When I finally jumped out of the plane strapped to "Hotty Scotty," my tandem instructor, the video depicted an almost frozen, panic-stricken version of myself. At that moment, I couldn't even scream, let alone relax.

A few seconds more into the video, you can see that I started to look at this situation and could almost read my mind.

I had certainly passed the point of changing my mind. So, I could choose to be petrified the whole time, or I could enjoy the ride. The moment I surrendered and allowed myself to be in the present, you could visibly see my arms relax and my hands open, and I am pretty sure you can see my mouth saying, "This is effing awesome!"

The prize is in the present. The present is received in the surrender of trying to control everything outside of ourselves. It is absurd that I could even consider that I could change the outcome once I jumped from that plane and yet we seem to feel like each experience we have can be controlled.

We are like back seat drivers thinking we are actually controlling the vehicle.

We don't control life. As much as we think we do, we have the ability to co-create experiences we would like to have, but we don't get to decide the how and the when. It's in these two things that we create suffering and discouragement. We may even have vision boards to keep us on the right-thinking track, but even the photos show the how in terms we can understand.

The financial abundance may come after the bankruptcy and in the depths of sorrow, we may surrender to the actual business or opportunity that will lead us to the dollars. The relationship we dream about may only come after we experience the pain of one that isn't aligned fully with ourselves. The answer to our health concerns may only come after we have felt the pain.

The secret is in experiencing it all. Relax and receive every moment in every second of our lives and experience it all. We can experience joy even amid the pain, the sorrow, and the things that don't seem to go our way.

Because everything that happens in our lives happens *for* us, not *to* us.

Relax, receive, breathe, and repeat.

So how in the world do you do this? You breathe, receive, and accept.

When you have a situation that comes up in your life that you would like to change, try to become the observer and watch how you react. Become unattached to the person it is happening to, because honestly, you aren't your body; you are simply experiencing this body and this current version of yourself. You aren't necessarily who you are, just as I am not really Wendy Bunnell. I am a soul and a spirit that is experiencing life as Wendy Bunnell. When I can view life in this manner, I realize that nothing is all that serious.

It may feel serious. When my whole body hurts—yep, it feels pretty serious. But if I can choose to relax into the experience, and get curious about the pain, I can sometimes understand that it is showing up for my benefit.

Byron Katie teaches a system called "The Work." She explains that the only time we suffer is when we believe a thought that argues with what is.

Let me share with you an example of a real world situation that occurred just today that depicts this in real time.

I finished writing this very book about 60 days ago. Since the very beginning, I set my sights on releasing my book and audio version on 11/11/22. I did everything in my power to ensure that this goal was met.

However, several things are preventing my audiobook from being released on that day, and it is possible that this book will not be able to get all of the pieces done in time to meet that deadline.

My thought earlier today was, "this shouldn't have happened. I did everything in my power to meet this goal, and I am mad as hell that it isn't happening the way it is supposed to.."

The fact is, the audiobook will not be able to be released on 11/11/22. That is the fact. There isn't room for that to change. The thought that is resisting what is happening is keeping me stuck and suffering.

Later in the day, my dear coach and mentor, Keira Poulsen, was able to gently guide me back to the truth. My audiobook will not be released on 11/11/22. That is a fact. As I shift my perspective on the truth, I noticed that my body relaxes and I stop resisting. My mind opens up to the possibilities and realizes that this new date opens up new marketing opportunities, and helps me to have another reason to talk about the book. Now I have two launch dates!

Surrendering is simply accepting what is.

The barriers that are preventing me from launching my audiobook on time, are also giving me an opportunity to rewrite this chapter you are reading. This was the only chapter I felt impressed to rewrite. I find it interesting that it is the chapter about surrender.

In perceiving life this way, the resistance goes away, and in its place is peace and a greater understanding of our circumstances. We can feel joy, even amid the chaos. We can choose to be happy, even when life is throwing us a curveball.

Surrender is crucial, especially when choosing to follow your heart to a new opportunity. The heart will always lead you to the next step, if you are open to trusting and receiving.

But most of us get hung up on the "how." If I choose another career, or decide to become an entrepreneur, what will it look like, how will I get there, and what specific blueprint will outline the steps necessary to get there?

And yet, we will never get the full set of instructions. It wasn't meant to be that way. We simply feel that gentle nudge, choose to surrender to it, and then allow the action steps to unfold as we trust the process.

And this lack of blueprints, this necessity to trust the process, is why so many of us will never take the chance to see what could happen if we chose our hearts instead of our minds.

A Course in Miracles says, "The ego analyzes; the Holy Spirit accepts. The appreciation of wholeness comes only through acceptance, for to analyze means to break down or separate out."

We can learn to accept life no matter what it throws out at us. It is a choice to either lean into fear and fight against something we will never win, or to simply lean the other way into love, see the beauty of the situation, accept the abundance of learning, growth, and new opportunities this event is giving us, and discover the truth of the situation.

Points to Ponder:

- Write down things in your life that aren't going in the manner you would have them show up. Now turn this around and write that they are supposed to be this way, because they are. How does that feel in your body? Do you feel lighter? Can you start to see the beauty in them? What are you learning?

- The next time you have stress, pause and relax. Breathe in and feel the emotion that rises in its fullness. Even with intense emotions, usually if you feel them in their fullness, they only feel uncomfortable for ninety seconds or so. You can do this, my friend. Breathe, receive, and allow the stress or emotion to move through you, instead of stuffing them down.

- Try to be the observer in your life for a moment. Next time you feel intense emotions, watch yourself and see how you react, what you choose, and what you think. Realize that you are not your body, your mind, or your emotions—you are simply aware of them. This takes practice but once you learn it, it will change your life.

- As you feel resistance for any part of your life, see if you can relax and choose to stand in the fact that this situation is *supposed* to happen versus taking the stance that it is not. It may not eliminate the pain right at that moment, but as you breathe and receive, you will start to see that the pain will eventually subside and you can return to a place of neutrality in which you can see things differently. The challenge may not go away, but you will see the suffering start to dissipate.

Chapter 18

TRUTH ABOUT FORGIVENESS

I used the hotel key to open up the room we were assigned. My husband and I had discovered only a few minutes earlier that the first room assigned was occupied, and so as luck would have it, the concierge upgraded us to a penthouse suite.

How fitting—it was our thirty-year anniversary.

Thirty years?? How could that be?! I had been married longer than I had been single.

And here we were celebrating that amazing milestone.

We wanted to go to Italy, but my health wouldn't allow it. This was the best we could do and so here we were in Park City. It's so interesting that thirty years previous, we had spent our honeymoon in this same mountain town.

As we entered the room, we noticed that we had been upgraded to a two-story, two-bedroom suite that overlooked the entire mountain. My jaw dropped. It was so beautiful.

A few hours later, we returned from a wonderful dinner and I played my mixtape that I had put together for him. We danced in front of the fireplace that was adorned on either side with those floor-to-ceiling windows.

Love.

All I could feel was love.

As we danced, so many memories filtered through my mind—the experiences of love that we had shared: the priceless memories of our children being born, the trips we'd taken, the places we had lived.

Whenever I need to recall the most loving moment in my life, I recall this memory. It was pure love that I felt for a man who had spent thirty years doing the best that he could, loving and showing up for a person he'd committed his life to.

And I saw him in all of his glorious, imperfect perfection. That love had helped us get through the hard times, the horrific times, and the madness.

And yet, this was the same man that I had begged God to show me a way to leave, not once, not twice, but hundreds of times.

Why would my experience be so different with the same person?

Love and forgiveness made the difference.

Learning to focus my attention on me and my healing allowed him to be free to do the same.

But it was through forgiveness that my perception changed.

In *A Course in Miracles* it says, "Forgiveness is the means by which we will remember. Through forgiveness the thinking of the world is reversed. The forgiven world becomes the gate of Heaven, because by its mercy we can at last forgive ourselves. Holding no one prisoner to guilt, we become free."

Freedom. Forgiveness allows us to be free, to start perceiving the world differently, to experience a very different world—one that isn't set on pain and suffering, but that allows for life force to run through us—and to wake up every cell in our bodies

I believe that Christ could heal with one touch because He was living a life in which forgiveness was seen in every action and as a result, He was radiating the vibration of love throughout His whole being.

Suffering and pain cannot be in the presence of such love. Thus, when the woman touched his robes and believed that she could be healed, she was. Simply being in His presence was enough.

Could you imagine what Planet Earth could be if we chose to forgive and step into love?

I believe one of the greatest mistakes we make in this life—stepping away from love and returning to resentment, frustration, and resistance—is self-betrayal.

There were countless times that I would return home from work and see my hungry family looking up at me wondering where their dinner was. I looked around the room and saw toys strewn all over the floor, and bodies sprawled out on the couch watching reruns of *SpongeBob*.

And I was pissed.

I felt so much anger in those moments, and felt sorry for myself on a regular basis.

I wondered why my life journey was not supported and yet, I was the one filling the gaps for everyone else. My cultural beliefs brought me back to the identity that I was "supposed" to fill, the one of wearing all the hats all at once. I was to be a taxi driver, a business woman, a lover, a mother, a teacher, a spiritual advisor, a cook, a maid—all the things *except* for who I really was: a woman in this lifetime with a divine identity.

I was so angry all of the time, and yet I didn't feel like a good person if I didn't accept these roles with graciousness and love. But the truth was, I wasn't happy about any of them.

I didn't feel like I "chose" any of them. At that point in my life, my life happened *to* me and not *for* me. And like a "good girl," I didn't say anything. I didn't speak up for my wants, my desires, my hopes, or my dreams, and so my heart closed for a very long time.

When your heart closes, you aren't open to intuition or answers. You are simply happy to sit in the shit you created because this muck gives you the validation that what you feel is real, and that you *do* have an unfortunate life—one that you didn't choose and one you didn't want.

And I was there; my heart was locked up tight for many, many years. This heart space is the receptor for our life force, and so I was continually tired, overwhelmed, frustrated, and unhappy.

Can you imagine living with me?

I can, because I begged to have some solace away from myself many, many times in my life. If I could have run, I would have sprinted away from my life, my body, my heart, and this reality I had created.

As I started to slowly open my heart every once in a while, I felt that happiness returned and I found a new perception of life.

I began to see things clearly and the outside world wasn't to blame for my plight. It was the internal dialogue and the way I had interpreted this existence that created my own personal hell.

The first thing I needed was to remember what I wanted, what I needed, and how I wanted to live this life. I deconstructed what I thought life was "supposed" to look like and began creating one that supported my soul without seeking the validation of others.

I chose to live a life that didn't include cleaning up after others all day, but instead one that included others helping and collaborating and working together in this life.

And so I spoke up.

And that was super uncomfortable at first. I didn't know how to do that, and even felt guilt and shame around the fact that I was finally having a say in this world.

My cultural upbringing showed me that women weren't supposed to say anything, and that a true woman of God served unceasingly without complaint and in that attitude would be found an abundance of energy to do all of His will.

Now that I am "tight" with God, I recognize that His Will is for me to co-create a life of joy and happiness and love. In that love I will have a heart wide open to share with others, and to hold space for their challenges and ups and downs in life.

As I started to open my solar plexus (our place of self-empowerment, right under the rib cage) once again, I chose to be brave and ask for the things that would create a space of love. Instead of asking everyone around me what they wanted for dinner, or where they wanted to go to eat, and then feeling bummed when they chose a place that wasn't conducive to my gluten free lifestyle, I spoke up.

Rather than saying, "I am good with whatever you decide" (sometimes I really do feel that way), I would say, "I would absolutely love a salmon salad at the Cliffside, with a big mason jar filled with an Arnold Palmer, and to sit on the deck overlooking the whole city."

And guess what? They were happy to oblige! My husband specifically loved to see me in pleasure and happiness. Men are hardwired to be thrilled when their spouse feels joy, and they get this inner peace that their role in empowered masculinity is serving their loving, empowered, divine, feminine wife.

They generally give up trying when nothing they do seems to improve the situation.

When I took back my desires and understood that I was in charge of my happiness, I let everyone else off the hook. This loving, open, and beautiful heart-opening space is where I live now.

The greatest source of pain comes from this belief that we don't have choices, that everything outside of us is the problem, and that if those things would change, we would be free.

Forgiveness is the antidote to this problem. And in order to fully forgive, it is mandatory that we take 100% responsibility for our lives. If we see that our life is not full of love and light and peace and joy, and we are experiencing destructive relationships, chaos, and financial burdens—we have the ability to change the story.

But first we need to change the belief in that story and find love instead of fear. The fear in that scenario is running the show and creating guilt and shame and suffering. But love can replace that by allowing the other players in your story to be set free.

A Course in Miracles says, "I give you to the Holy Spirit as part of myself. I know that you will be released, unless I want to use you to imprison myself. In the name of freedom I choose your release, because I recognize that we will be released together."

What does this mean?

Well, it's a three-part process.

The first part is to realize that the problem you are perceiving is made up in your mind. You created a story around the problem. For instance, if my husband isn't helping me with dishes, I create a story around him not respecting me and using me to avoid responsibility. The first step is realizing that a story was created. The moment I move out of that story and realize I had made it up in my head, I start going back to the truth.

The second part is to choose how to view the story. At the beginning of that experience, I have two choices: I can move toward either fear or love.

If I choose to believe that I am "right" and that this story is indeed true, I will separate from love and become stuck in fear, which brings to me self-pity, victimization, and unhappiness.

If I choose to discover what I would like more of, and ask God to help me see what else is possible, I may come to the decision to simply ask for help. If I truly want help, I can ask in a loving way: "I would love some help in the kitchen. Would you consider helping me?"

And when met with love and an open heart, nine out of ten times, he (and most individuals) will gladly step up to the plate.

And if the answer is no, perhaps I could open up to the fact that he is making a choice based on a whole other set of reasons, and as soon as I end my story of victimization, I might be open to understanding that as well. I can also make the choice to complete the dishes and become absorbed in the experience. I can feel the sudsy water on my hands, feeling the warmth and wonder of the water. I can watch the dishes go from dirty to beautifully clean and feel the sense of accomplishment that comes after doing the task and completing it.

Now some of you may feel like this process means that you are setting yourself up for being used and treated poorly. In actuality, this process opens your heart and you can see with clarity. If there are reasons to be concerned about a toxic situation, you will know and be led to the proper next steps in order to heal the relationship or put up boundaries and end the cycle of abuse.

But it can't be done when we are stuck in our stories.

It is essential to look outside of those stories and recognize the guiltlessness that exists in all of us. Our stories and perceptions about occurrences in this life are what create the guilt, shame, blame, and hurt feelings.

If the world could find this place of love and forgiveness, we wouldn't ever offend others because they wouldn't create a story around the words you choose or say. We wouldn't have to take down statues, or change college mascot names in order to avoid hurting someone's feelings, because our emotional intelligence would surpass any event in our life. We could let that situation pass us by, because we are in a place of forgiveness even as we start to see that there isn't actually anything to forgive.

Even when uncoupling and boundaries are necessary in a relationship, if it is done in a state of love, we will always win. The shift of what *A Course in Miracles* states is one of allowing the Holy Spirit to move through us and allow us to stay in love.

The Bible tells us to "love thy neighbor" and *A Course in Miracles* shows us how to do that.

The last step is to surrender to the shift that will occur within. This step will not take place *by* you, but *through* you. You will most likely feel this through an energetic shift in your body and mind. You can call it by many names: the Holy Spirit, Jesus Christ, God, Allah, Universe, Source Energy. In reality, the name doesn't matter because it is all the same energy that will change your heart and open it up to all of the joy, happiness, and peace you have been seeking.

I believe that even more important than forgiving others, the greatest opportunities are in forgiving ourselves.

As I started shifting away from my faith of origin over the last few years, I felt an incredible amount of shame, guilt, and darkness, and so I moved away from so many people I loved. I separated myself from anyone who was active in that religion because it was so painful to visit the emotions that I was experiencing.

I would see church buildings and feel this stab of guilt within my gut. I would walk by missionaries and wonder if my decision would lead to my eternal damnation. I would see an old church friend at the store and avoid talking to them.

I created a story around the reasons I was justified in leaving, and started to look at "those people" with judgment and disregard. Many of those individuals were my own family members. I struggled with being around them, not because they were showing up differently, but because of my feelings of inadequacy and even superiority with my newfound beliefs. And while those new perceptions were helping me to feel free, the story was keeping me away from the actual truth and sense of belonging that I desired.

After telling my mother about my decision to go on another spiritual path, I felt so much pain and shame that I experienced a fibromyalgia attack for almost two months. It happened right around the time that I went on a spring break trip and caused me to not enjoy a single moment on that trip.

I was drowning in fear. I was so enmeshed with the thoughts and stories that didn't allow me to be free from suffering.

The very reason I chose to leave the Church was so that I could find freedom and peace. And here I was, creating my own version of hell right here on this earth.

It took me several months to navigate and dismantle those stories. As I opened my heart up to the truth and saw that I was guiltless, just like everyone else on Planet Earth, I started to see things clearly and without the perception of guilt.

I used the three-part strategy of dismantling the story, leaning into love instead of fear, and feeling the shift that comes when we let go of the lies.

Freedom is here because of forgiveness. I simply let myself free of the tangle of lies I had created within myself. I could forgive because in reality, there wasn't anything to forgive. There was simply love. Love for a woman who was starting to choose herself. Love for a life of her creation. Love for humanity and family and connections that were hers for a lifetime of experiences and memories.

Forgiveness is freedom, my friends.

Set yourself free. That freedom is yours for the taking.

Points to Ponder:

- The next time you find yourself feeling like a victim, stop and pay attention to the dialogue that is happening in your mind. What stories have you created? Write down the stories you have created so you can see them in real life.
- Use the three-part method once you discover your story:
    - Recognize the stories you made up, and realize they were indeed made up by you.
    - Choose to lean into fear and the need to be "right" or choose to lean into love and set yourself free.
    - The shift in your frequency is going to come from the Universal force of light and love. You don't need to do anything for this step; you simply receive the freedom in that experience.

Chapter 19

TRUTH ABOUT JUDGMENT

I asked God right before drifting off to sleep, "God, what would it feel like to be free of judgment? How would I see things differently? How would I connect to myself and to others?"

This thought permeated my thoughts in a loop for several hours and even filtered through my dreams. A few hours later, I awoke and felt impressed to listen to the tinnitus in my ears, the constant ringing that has been a part of my life for the past five years.

A gentle prompting encouraged me to focus intently on that sound and to focus my attention on my third eye. After several minutes, I felt a shift that startled me a little at first, but another prompt coaxed me to relax and surrender.

At that moment, my headspace started to tingle and I felt like effervescent bubbles were being released in my body from my spine up toward my head and out of my crown. Again, my natural tendency was to be a bit alarmed but I heard my own voice say, "Let's do this."

And then it happened . . .

The glorious rapture of divine energy coursed through my entire body. It felt like it wrapped me in an eternal buzzing of peace that vibrated at such a high level that I could feel love, which I finally allowed to run through me.

"This is what it feels like to be free of judgment," the familiar voice said.

I felt a warm glow fill my entire body and mind. There was an incredible lightness that replaced the heavy energy that used to reside in my heart space, my shoulders, my neck, and especially my gut.

"You have placed judgment on the world, yourself, and others. This judgment has placed a veil over your eyes so that you cannot see the full beauty of the world. You cannot see your full divinity, or that of others, because you have a need to understand and make sense of the world instead of simply being in the world. This judgment has caused you every bit of pain, suffering, and worry you have had. You created this world of ugliness because you felt impressed to justify every emotion and label your feelings and thoughts and experiences as good or bad. You see, nothing is good or bad, right or wrong, black or white. They are simply experiences, along with your full capacity to be in this amazing body, and the ability to feel emotions. Isn't it glorious?" my divine guide taught.

I filtered through my life again and remembered the stories—the stories of challenge, the stories of pain, the stories of suffering, the stories of sorrow.

They all shared one common element . . . judgment.

This judgment created my feelings of shame, blame, guilt, and inferiority.

I started sharing these stories at the beginning of this book. My suffering in my dad's death came from a place of guilt around my inability to save him from his own pain. I jumped back and forth between wanting to save him and needing to condemn him for the painful choices he made. It was from my judgment that the shame permeated my whole being and consumed me, imprisoning me in a place of despair and riddling me with anxiety and depression.

I moved toward sharing about my miscarriage. I felt this guilt that I had somehow brought this upon myself after my sister's babies died. This guilt held me hostage and drove me to blame Western medicine, pharmaceutical companies, and myself for not listening to my inner voice.

My career was a perceived cage that I had surrounded myself in because I believed that I had to do life in a certain manner. I placed judgment on what type of life was acceptable and what life was unacceptable. I worked myself into the ground to prove that I was more than the shame and guilt that seemed to follow me around all of the time.

I held onto my sexual trauma because I felt the need to punish myself for having been in a position to experience the loss of the one thing that every person in my life said was most precious above all—my virtue, my virginity. So I hung onto shame and guilt in an effort to redeem myself. I saw a connection between the intensity of the judgment and the amount of pain I experienced in my life.

It all made perfect sense now.

When I released judgment and returned to truth and love, I returned to connection.

I returned to connection with myself and then with those I judged, and then with the divine love that exists behind the shame.

And in doing so, I set myself free.

When I stepped out of judgment, I returned to love and aligned myself with the Divine.

That is why I felt so light when I was free of judgment. That is why I felt so connected to all things, because I was seeing them in their truth instead of in the lies that I had fabricated along the way.

In the next moment, the story of Adam and Eve filtered through my mind.

"Adam and Eve did not drive themselves out of the Garden of Eden due to eating an apple. They placed a veil over their eyes in the moment that they perceived that they had sinned by eating the apple. They judged themselves for the first time in that moment, and with this judgment they experienced shame. Judgment and shame divided them and cast them out of my presence. I was always right here, but they couldn't feel me or see me because their shame created a different world, a world of pain, suffering, opposites" the divine voice explained.

I had created a different world. I had created a world of pain and suffering and chaos and heartache because I judged everything in my life.

Even judging something to be good could bring upon us guilt and shame. For instance, if I released weight and perceived myself as beautiful and sexy, the moment I put weight on, I would feel even worse than before. I would berate myself with statements like, "You can never get this right. What the hell is wrong with you?" The judgment that my weight made me better or worse was what caused the pain; the weight was simply the place of judgment.

And I noticed I did this all of the time. There were good foods and bad foods. There were successful people and individuals that seemed to live off of others and the government. There were faithful and religious people, and those that were rebellious. Some individuals were kind and some preyed on people.

But the bulk of my judgment was on myself. I was too carefree, I wasn't responsible, I didn't make good decisions, I didn't love others enough, I didn't spend enough time with my family. I was selfish, I was broken—my brain was broken, I was mentally ill, I had a broken body.

Just reading those words is heavy.

I created my own version of hell with my judgments.

And now I felt what it was like to be free of judgment. Even if it was for a short period of time, it allowed me to feel what it was like to be full of love instead. I felt the weight of the world lift off of my shoulders because I understood that I couldn't get things wrong; I simply got to experience it all if I chose, or experience only a few things if I decided to go that direction. My life was of my own creation. And if I chose to be curious instead of creating senseless meaning, I would invite heaven back into my life.

So how do I get myself out of judgment? How do I relearn how to do life?

I start with awareness. In the book, *Body Whispering*, Dr. Dain Heer explains that it can be as easy as asking yourself a question. A statement that he suggests is, "Interesting. Isn't that an interesting point of view . . . that is my point of view."

Simply understanding that your life journey is your interpretation of each experience allows you to realize that it is simply your point of view and that you don't have to choose a meaning anymore. It simply is.

Each time I use this statement, I feel a lightning within my system. I no longer add the weight of judgment into my soul when I choose to be aware instead of judgmental.

In terms of past judgment, the acts of forgiveness and gratitude can set it free.

I can choose to forgive myself for hating my body and then shift back into gratitude for what it has done for me.

I can choose to look at my muffin top with disdain and disgust, or I can look at it and recognize that it held five babies and created life. This same place in my body has digested countless meals, and thoughts, and emotions. My body has never left me; it has always shown up for me.

In that realization, love pours through me and I return back to the truth.

As I marinated in the experience I had just had, I realized how incredibly challenging I have made this life. I have judged myself harshly, judged others around me, and painted an ugly picture of the world for most of my life. Sure there were moments of happiness, but I would return to the trauma and judgment of the past after enjoying only a few moments of respite.

I started to laugh out loud.

Are you kidding me? This is how easy it can be to return to love? I simply forgive the past, have an awareness of my judgment in the present, and exercise gratitude to see what is really true?

That's it?

I laughed from my entire being. I had indeed made this life a more serious affair than it needed to be.

This chapter was intentionally held for me to write last. I wasn't ready to write it until this very moment, because I didn't understand what was holding me hostage to all my pain and suffering. I knew that perception had a part of this pattern, but I didn't understand the weight of what judgment had done to me throughout my lifetime.

This discovery is like a lightening, an awakening, a return to love.

I believe that the world is starting to be open to seeing the lies. And as we do so collectively, we will be walking into the light together. We will be translated back into the miraculous beings we have always been and realize that we are one.

I can see clearly now.

I am home.

I am back home with myself and the truth of all things.

Welcome home my friend. Welcome back to YOUR truth.

Points to Ponder:

- Become aware of when you judge a situation, place, person, or thing. You will most likely find that judgment has ruled your life up until this point. But with this new awareness, you can step into curiosity. Be patient with yourself as you learn how to become aware. Don't judge your judgment (LOL).

- When you start to judge, turn that into a curiosity. Isn't it interesting that this is your point of view? It is so interesting how you view the world. So interesting.

- Try using gratitude when you start feeling judgment, especially when it is directed at you. Feel the incredible shift of going from fear (judgment) into love (acceptance and gratitude).

Chapter 20
TRUTH FOUND

I drive up the dirt road to the home that will be the sanctuary that will hold space for me to complete this beautiful project that I have been spiritually assigned to bring to the world.

The book will be born this weekend. It is a book filled with words that are not of my own creation: words that only made sense to me because they are shared through my journey, my story, and my life—the only life-journey story I know; words that hold promise to more peace, more happiness, more joy.

I am humbled, and I am honored to have been the vessel for the truth to be channeled through. Nothing has brought me more joy than this, so I couldn't understand why, over the past week, I have felt so much anxiety, depression, and sadness.

The emotions welled up inside . . . and I chose to feel them all.

I began asking questions as I got curious and compassionate. My soul had a desire to understand and provide the unconditional love that my emotions needed.

"Anxiety, what are you telling me?" my soul asked.

"I am afraid of being seen," anxiety said.

Soul: Why are you afraid, sweetheart?

Anxiety: Because not everyone will understand me and this book—especially my family—and it won't feel good when they reject me.

Soul: Breathe. . . .Okay, you are afraid of your family rejecting you. That is pretty big stuff, isn't it? Back in the beginning of the world, if your tribe rejected you—you died. Are you afraid of death?

Anxiety: No, I am not afraid of death, but I am afraid of losing love, of their hearts closing up to me. It will crush me.

Soul: That will probably hurt . . . If they close their hearts and reject you, what will you do?

Soul: I will love myself. I can only love myself. And I know how to receive love from the source of all love.

Anxiety: So will you lose love if they reject you?

Soul: No. I will learn to accept and receive love from the endless supply that is available to me. Interesting . . . interesting that my point of view is that others will reject me. That is *my* point of view.

Truth found. Moving on . . .

Okay next?

Soul: Depression, why are you sad, my friend. How are you feeling?

Depression: Not good. I think I might die.

Soul: You might die? Why is that?

Depression: If you become successful then you will probably experience what your Dad and your Grandma experienced and they both died; they both suffered greatly, and I don't want that for you.

Soul: Breathe . . . Am I trying to get success to fill a place in my soul that seems to be missing? No. I know who I am and it doesn't matter if one person or one thousand people read this book. The book has healed me in the process of writing it, and so it has all been worth it—every single word, every single minute of writing. It is a testament to the truth of the words. I am whole and I don't need the external world to validate that for me anymore. Interesting . . . you believe that your relatives died from success—interesting point of view. That is *my* point of view.

Truth exposed.

Okay next . . . stress?

Stress: You have no idea where this will take you. You retired from your career for hell's sake! Where are you going to make money? Did you forget that it takes money to eat? You are so incredibly irresponsible.

Soul: So you feel like this is irresponsible.

Stress: Yes!! We need to plan our future and make sure that we have money and means and a place to sleep!

Soul: Have you ever been without a meal or a place to sleep?

Stress: No, but the way you are acting, we will start being hungry soon!!

Soul: Breathe . . . The truth is that I have always been given means to take care of myself, and we will continue to have what we need in order to live and thrive. That may look differently than today, but won't that be exciting to see how it comes into our lives?

Stress: I don't like surprises, and I don't like not knowing, and I like to be in control.

Soul: You have never been in control, my friend. You are actually sitting in the backseat right now, barking orders and hoping someone will listen. You feel so out of sorts because you want to have that control, and yet you will never have it. Isn't it time for you to relax for once and surrender to what is?

Stress: Whatever.

Soul: I have compassion for you—you are human and I am divine, and I don't need to have the answers. I have faith and trust and love that everything is always happening in my highest and best and this is no different. Relax and receive, my friend. Relax and receive. Interesting that you judge your new career as irresponsible. That is *my* point of view.

Last truth exposed. I breathe in a sigh of relief knowing that I have returned to a space of love and relax into the process of writing the final pages of the book you are now holding in your hands.

This is a process I choose to experience—emotions, thoughts, and beliefs that used to consume me but now simply flow through me. I become aware of the judgment and my point of view and then expose the truth. They teach me the lessons I need to learn and then I can return to peace once again.

So if you were wondering if I had multiple personalities before, now you can confirm your suspicions with these last few pages.

It's not that I actually have different personalities; it is that I have discovered that I am not really that voice inside my head, or the emotions coursing through my body, or even my body, for that matter. I am a separate soul that resides inside of my body, feeling all of the emotions and stimuli that flow through it. I get to experience what it is like to be fully human and fully divine at the same time.

That, my friend, is my truth.

And it is glorious.

I used to spend my time fighting a war with each one of those parts. Most of my life was spent doing that, but now that I am aware, I spend more time being an observer in that curious and compassionate stance than I do in participating in the battle.

And because of that awareness, I can experience it and not find any meaning or contrive stories about that space. It is usually the stories and judgment that create the grief and suffering.

I read the stories that I've shared in this book, and I realize how challenging I made this simple life we lead, and how the stories brought so much unnecessary suffering. But I also realize that it is okay that I have chosen to learn that way. Every single experience and lesson has come in perfect timing and in the perfect way.

I have discovered that the external world is just to be experienced and not taken so seriously all of the time. It is actually quite entertaining when you view it from that perspective.

And now it is your turn.

You picked up this book for a reason. Your heart led you to read it so that you could also start to wake up and remember the forgotten pieces of your divinity.

I have such reverence and respect for you, my friend.

You have arrived at the end, or perhaps it is just the beginning . . . as you discover that the truth was always inside of you. That the world outside is a fake shell in comparison to the immense love and vast knowledge of insight that exists inside us and through us.

No to-do lists assigned, no endless hours of things that you need to study or do, just a lifetime of coming back to yourself.

For some that may be as quick as making the decision to remember and come back to the self, but for most of us it is a process of peeling off layers of lies and untangling the programs that have blinded us to what is and what always has been.

Let's clear up a few expectations before you embark on this journey.

Don't create any expectations at all.

Your journey is just that . . . your journey.

No one else can predict what you'll feel and what you'll see and the experiences that you'll have along the way.

Most likely you will still have days where you are feeling intense emotions and you will have the opportunity to feel them, and maybe even interact with them. You may even still call them "bad days."

But this is what we came down here for—to experience life in all its fullness, colors, and grandeur.

Even as I was the person channeling this book, I will undoubtedly have opportunities to remember my human side, the insecurities, and get swept back into people-pleasing mode from time to time. Or not . . . it all depends on what I choose.

It doesn't matter how, it just matters that you show up and experience everything. You can choose to love that ride and not take it seriously or you can get into the pit of suffering if you want to.

Or perhaps . . . you can choose you. You can choose love. You can choose to step away from judgment and return to truth and you can choose your version of divinity to call upon at any time.

And when we remember to open our heart spaces, we are connected to all. This way of being will help the collective to come back to their heart space as well. The greatest gift I can give to humanity is to come back to me. The greatest gift you can give to humanity is to come back to you.

Let's hold each other's hands and walk each other home.

Truth. Freedom. Peace.

It is where we have always been and where we will always be.

We have been in a long, deep slumber of distractions that have shown us that we need to be a certain someone, live a certain way, have a certain lifestyle, and have proof that we did it correctly.

But the reality is that we have never had to *do* anything.

We have never had to do anything except to live, love, experience, and enjoy the journey.

The suffering we experience is there because we have created it. It is a hard pill to swallow, but it is true. When we take 100% responsibility for every part of our lives, we will begin to see how to undo the misery, the heartache, the pain, and the suffering that we have created.

Each section of truths in this book has the power to shed another layer of pain, another layer of the lies that we built up around us.

And there is so much help from the other side. There are angels and helpers just waiting for you to ask them for help. Simply ask and ye shall receive.

Religious organizations over the millennia have tried to depict a God that we should fear, a God that we should avoid.

But my God is a God of peace. My God is a God of love. My God is a God of health. My God is a God of freedom.

Anything contrary to those statements are made from fear.

And right now, we can all feel fear. We can feel it through our media channels, through our government, through the economy. We understand and feel fear and therefore we put the armor around our heart to protect it from the outside world.

But it is through our heart that we heal, and that healing will transfer to your family, to your friends, and finally, to the world and the collective.

It is time to come back to love, to exist in love, and to remember who we are at the core of our soul and our being.

It is time to return to our truth and step into the next realm of consciousness. The Christ consciousness is arriving right now. It is calling all of us back home to end the cycle of suffering that we all have become accustomed to.

It is time to return to love.

Truth and Dare: are you willing to live your truth in a fake world?

Poem

THE WARRIOR CRY OF THE HEART

The outside world held up a broken mirror
It showed a splintered version that wasn't true
Another voice kept gently nudging
To show you the vision of what's true
Once you caught a glimpse of the truth
You grabbed the mirror and melted it in the fire
The fire that was within and was allowed to unleash
And it burnt the lies, the programs, and beliefs
And all that was left was the truth
Your truth
And nothing was more magical than the fierce warrior within
And the warrior cried out in victory to the world
Never to be quieted again
The Warrior Cry of the Heart has begun

PROLOGUE

The book you hold in your hands has changed my very DNA as I have written it. Every single truth that I shared with you unfolded another layer of understanding for my own personal life.

It has taken me through every emotion imaginable. I have had the opportunity to visit all of them, and understand the magnitude of their greatness. I am in awe of the goodness of life, of emotions, of experiences, of connection, and most of all the goodness of love.

Each chapter in this book led me closer to my own truth. Each chapter led me to my own acceptance, gratitude, and forgiveness of the insecurities and misunderstandings of my journey up until the present.

Through forgiveness, compassion, and stepping out of judgment, I have found love on an elevated level. I am in awe of the goodness of God. I am in awe of the power each of us holds when we get out of our own way.

Along this journey I found tools that would bring greater light and knowledge that will help me and those that I teach. These tools have helped me to stay within the confines of truth and love.

This journey led me to a new love-of-creation video. Telling my story visually was one of the most beautiful creative processes I have ever experienced.

The miracles that occurred during that creative process showed me how true surrender and trust could bring me to the right people, places, and vision to create something that was way beyond my human abilities. I watch the #time2heal video (click here) and cry every single time. Every. Single. Time.

That video led to a movement. I believed in my human mind that the video would simply promote my book. It only took one look at the video to realize that this was much more than any marketing tool; this was a movement taking the masses past #metoo and into #time2heal. My heart is humbled knowing that I was a part of this movement.

I also discovered the beauty of plant medicine during the process of writing this book. Mother called me home to remember the truth of all things and to expand my mind past what I am visually seeing and what is beyond the layer of lies that I have created. I cannot express my gratitude knowing that all we need and all we have is right here.

I later learned about technology that helps with emotional intelligence. This technology will help open up understanding to the truth of emotions like nothing else I have ever seen. Again, I would never have been led to this place of understanding had I not said "yes" to this book and this experience. This new technology will be spread through an app that I will be helping to market to individuals. I will also be working with a nonprofit organization called the MECA project, which will help teens and young adults access the app free of charge. It is time to help our newest generation to learn the beauty of their emotions.

I also have been invited to create future projects that will help remind us of the beauty of connection and community.

Next June, I will be collaborating with the amazing Laurel Huston to help thirty-two women heal from the trauma of the past in a five day/four night healing experience like no other. The power of women can indeed facilitate change and healing, and these five days will transcend us all to the next level.

And Burning Woman . . . all I have to do is utter the words into the Universe and people look up and ask what it is all about.

Picture this: a community that focuses on the tenets of giving and serving through their spiritual gifts with no expectation for reciprocation. However, it is encouraged for everyone to receive by asking and discovering new modalities of understanding and healing from others in the community that hold the answers. It's a community built around self-reliance and self-love.

This community will gather in 2023 in Cedar City from September 15- September 18, 2023.

It will be focused on that community spirit and have experiences that help us to remember our inner child by playing in the man-made lake (complete with waterslides), enjoying the zip lines, and dancing to music emanating from the stadium stage, which is set in the middle of 200 acres of beauty.

We will burn the things of the past that hold us back and leave renewed with our passion and purpose re-lighted and renewed.

All of this because I chose in. I chose to listen to my heart. I chose to listen to the Divine Spirit of knowing. I chose me. I love me, which allows me to love humanity.

Are you feeling the pull to collaborate and join me? You can find me and all of my beautiful and juicy creations on my website. The QR code will be found on the next page, or simply type in my name as the URL and join me in this crusade to unfold truth and light and discover that all of the answers are found within.

Namaste and Satnam, my friends.

This is just the beginning . . .

TRUTH & DARE
RESOURCES

It is my core desire to assist you on your journey to discovering your own personal truth.

I have designed programs, women's circles, retreats, and the Burning Woman events to support you in this evolution of discovery.

My sincere hope is that you will at least join us in our FB community where we can provide a safe place to land. It is a place where you will find women using their beautiful divine feminine energy to nurture, listen, and advocate for one another.

You can find links to all of these resources on one page.

This will constantly be updated to provide you with the latest and greatest offerings that my team and I create on your behalf.

Or...Click Here

Namaste and Satnam, my friends

ACKNOWLEDGEMENTS

I would like to express a heartfelt thank you to the hundreds of individuals who have helped me understand my own truth. There are too many of you who have made a profound impact on my life, and so I shy away from naming you one by one as I most certainly would forget an important name. If you are wondering if you are one of them, yes my friend, you are.

To my publisher, mentor, and friend who taught me how to channel this book, thank you. Keira, you have made a profound impact on my life. I will never be the same after writing this book.

To my family who pivot with my ever-changing life, even though you most likely get whiplash from the crazy ride with me, you still find joy and exhilaration in the journey with me. Thank you for taking this ride with me and not getting off the crazy train.

To my husband of 33 years, thank you from the depths of my heart for being my greatest advocate and biggest cheerleader. You are indeed my soulmate and partner for life.

To my readers, thank you for reading my book. I hope it has made a positive change in your life. I pray that something will shift inside of you, bringing you closer to your heart and soul and helping you remember the magnitude of your greatness that has always been there awaiting your discovery once again.

ABOUT THE AUTHOR

Wendy Bunnell is a serial entrepreneur of over thirty years. She loves to pair her passion for business with the ability to make an impact on the world and help others in their journey.

She has learned through the years how to create with divine feminine energy and design a life that is abundant in all areas.

She has learned that connecting with yourself, others, and the Divine is the path to discovering truth. In Wendy's opinion, the key to happiness is staying in your truth and away from judgment, which leads to peace, fulfillment, joy, and true unconditional love.

Her heart belongs to six children, twelve grandchildren, and her soulmate of 33 years.

Did you love this book?

Don't forget to leave a review!

Each review matters… a lot!

It would be amazing if you could head over to Amazon, or wherever you purchased this book and leave a review! Thank you, thank you, thank you.

Much Love, Wendy

Made in the USA
Las Vegas, NV
13 November 2022